Life Is What Happens ... at *Play*

A True Story That Reminds Us of the Magic We Can Discover through Our Inherent Ability to Play

Hannah Lee

BALBOA.
PRESS
A DIVISION OF HAY HOUSE

Balboa Press books may be ordered through booksellers or by contacting:

Balboa Press
A Division of Hay House
1663 Liberty Drive
Bloomington, IN 47403
www.balboapress.com
1 (877) 407-4847

Print information available on the last page.

ISBN: 978-1-5043-4324-4 (sc)
ISBN: 978-1-5043-4325-1 (e)

Balboa Press rev. date: 11/10/2015

Contents

Dedication This Book is for CACAO

"An adventurous soul he was, and brave too! Cacao sailed the high seas and kept us going the night through in the rough and tumble of the drenched cockpit floor of our tiny little bathtub sailboat! When all was said and done, twenty hours or so later, the three of us had reached safety, weathered and worn, but with considerably more character, and certainly more appreciation for life than before our frightening all night journey across the big black sea!"

"He should have died much sooner!" I always said. "I swear on my grave that cat had twelve lives...not nine!"

This book is in loving memory of Cacao, rescued down south while we were sailing. He was one very special animal soul who changed the lives of two people, bringing them ever so much love and joy. I often wonder who really was rescued – us or him! He died at the age of seven with an enlarged heart, the doctors said - one very large heart indeed!

As a general lesson, Cacao taught me this: Be aware of those who, through fate or free will, come into your life for "a season, a reason, or a lifetime". Sometimes those special souls are the animals we love the most!

Acknowledgements

Inspired by new age and self-help authors Eckhart Tolle, Esther and Jerry Hicks, Dan Millman, Melody Beattie, Elizabeth Gilbert and Barbara Ann Brennan together with the support of my close-at-heart family in Canada whom I adore, my truthful and patient mother and my two beautiful sisters who all helped me in their own loving ways on my journey to writing and finishing this book, I truly have been given the opportunity and the medium of safety, love and encouragement necessary to explore ideas, feelings, emotions and realities in an honest and nonjudgmental environment, and I am so grateful for that.

Next to those across the miles whose never failing love has carried me, my closest family consists of a frenzy of felines who have given me devoted understanding and undying love! They have been there for me through tears and laughter and spent many nights putting up with my crazy quirky thoughts and antics when writing this book. Without them and the listening hearts of my good friends along the way, I could not have had the capacity to see this book to the end! A true lover of animals, I have spent much of my time seeking out homeless cats, rescuing them and having them spayed and neutered whenever possible. It is partially the efforts of other animal welfare groups who have inspired me to continue to write, for if they can accomplish so much, I can simply complete one book! I am a true supporter of Animals Asia in their efforts to free the Moon Bears from their captivity and horrible suffering, and the World Society for the Protection of Animals (WSPA) in their endeavors to protect and prevent animal cruelty. Their websites are provided below.
www.wspa-international.org www.animalsasia.org

Finally, I would like to acknowledge two people whom I have only encountered briefly along the way: First, Dr. Stuart Brown, Founder and Director of the National Play Institute in California, for giving me the capacity and new inspiration on the importance of play in our lives; second, Gaye Facer, a sweet woman whom I bumped into at poolside on my travels in Nicaragua. We immediately connected, chatted for little less than two hours and being a writer, editor and literary consultant herself, we reconnected as a result of my seeking out her professional advice. I am honored to have been given time by both of these busy people! Thank you for helping me on my way to writing a successful non-fiction book!

Prologue

So there I was....sitting in a natural hot spring, soaking my aching muscles and wounded soul.

And I came to wonder just how small we all are. How do we find ourselves in a special place at any given moment in time? Is there a purpose, a meaning to it? Does each of us fit into the puzzle to make it eventually complete? Or does it just happen by chance, with no further necessity for thought? Is it spontaneous insignificance or nothing by chance?

As I slowly soaked into the mineral pool, which I had just hiked two hours to find, I found myself absorbing the totality of the energy around me. And play began to happen.

The clouds were jiggling like jello, and as I giggled out loud at their life-like movements, I began to see a face. It looked like Popeye! I smiled, and then laughed out loud again.

Meanwhile, it looked as though a bird was busy watching me watching the clouds. As I noticed the magic of the beauty and life around me, suddenly nothing else mattered. Everything I had experienced and taken along with me up until now was gone! Vanished! I laid back, finally and completely trusting the clay ridden earth beneath me. As my head grew heavy on the pillow of rock, I could feel the tension and fatigue in my neck, and then my back muscles began to sink in deeper, trusting further....and I was in the moment.

Confusion

I sobbed....I cried...I felt....I lied....
I'm blessed...I'm confused...I feel....everything....nothing...
Sadness...love....emotion.....thoughts. . .blank. . .
I'm scared – terrified! Who will fall mayhem to my heart next? Who will fall prey to my path? What innocent soul will open his heart up so lovingly to me? I will love in illusion for a little while, and then turn him away - to darkness - when I showed him light.
I sobbed....I cried....I felt....I lied.

Who Am I? Who am I to deserve so much love? Have you ever felt torn between people you loved? Ripped apart at the seams between lovers, companions, soul mates? My head hurts. My heart aches.

It's called confusion. How does one decide? How is one to know what is best for the self, the other, the universe?

Mine is not the "typical" challenge...or is it? How many people have the chance to fall in love with more than one person at a time? Then how many are opened and honest about it? It is very painful for someone who hasn't a clue how to deal with even a little love, let alone love from two such genuine souls.

So what is happening to me? I am sobbing in confusion and desperation for lack of direction and solution. Oh my God! It's so frustrating to be loved so much! Can't these people just abandon me? Why can't they just walk away - just like everyone else ever did?

Just walk away! It would make everything so much easier. It would be what I know!

I am finding it hard to breathe! But wait, I remember once someone told me that breath is life. When we play, we breathe. Yes, I will retreat to play! That surely will help me to figure it all out!

"Molly, just breathe", says some sweet little inner voice.

Angels Among Us

There are angels! Angels are everywhere! They are all around me - in the stars, the clouds, the sea, the sand, the trees, the birds, the wind. Some might call them God and some faint of religion, but those of spirit, might call them part of a universal love. Whatever they are in the human language, they are ever there! And when we are most confused or most desperate, even sometimes most fulfilled and elated, they are there! They just show up! They don't ask what time it is or what day of the week. They just surface!

I can recall a few experiences, at times in dreams, and other times when I had partaken in some mood altering activities. Still, there were other moments when angels would appear through auditory means in the wind when I could clearly hear them whispering my name.

I was looking at a picture of my sweet older sister, Monica, she had sent me when I was going through a major crisis in my life, an impending divorce. The picture was absolutely beautiful and appalling too! It made me feel ill and made me smile at the same time. Here were three beautiful women - very young girls at the time – three, four and seven perhaps. We were three beautiful souls, all with arms in the air, looking ready to conquer the world. Oh how pictures can lie! We were all so innocent and terrified! An alcoholic father, a mother who was doing her best to coexist with codependency, and three beautiful souls who were looking to her for EVERYTHING - love, need fulfillment and basic care. Little did we or she know that it was much more complicated than that.

As I gazed deeper into the picture, mesmerized by its realness, lo and behold, there were three angels, right there - in that picture – with halos and wings! Oh my God! It was us - Monica, Maxine and Molly!

A Child's World

I never asked for my world. I was merely born into it to learn the lessons not yet wrought from past lives.

I was so safe. I wish I could remember that feeling - so very safe in my mama's womb....or was I? I was actually the result of an unplanned, unwanted pregnancy, with parents much too young and confused to ever love and adore children of their own. Both were bordering on issues that had been passed down through the generations and, of course, results of their learned behaviors from past lives and lessons put before them. They say we are partial products of our womb experiences. There are qualities we all have that go unexplained, even with deep inner work and self-reflection. So it is important to be aware of this in order to let go of those things that we cannot change or never know. In fact, we only have a limited cup of free will. Before we are born, we choose to enter a womb in order to bare our soul existence in this lifetime - in order to learn the lessons we have come back to learn to essentially help us evolve. As embryos, we develop into something called a child - a little baby that comes through another human being of choice, to help heal the self and the people through whom we came - in order to ultimately contribute to healing the universe in all of its suffering, joy, pain and pleasure - a process called evolution.

I used to cry terribly when my mom would leave me to go off to work. She always did her best, being a single mom, to leave me and my sisters with the best possible care.

Mrs. G was one of those wonderful ladies who scared the living hell out of me with her big bulgy eyes! But I always knew she'd never hurt me. She just wasn't the prettiest woman to look at! And to a child, everyone is scary! I always felt so tiny and helpless in her presence. And then there was Nick and Mary - true earth angels for my desperate, single, trying–to– make–ends-meet mother. They were a sweet little Ukrainian couple with hearts of gold. They would spoil us rotten with chocolate cake and whip cream and brandy for our sore throats!

When my mom met Mr. A, *my* very essence - my inner child - was taken over with fear and shame. I was so impressionable, innocent and ignorant at that time, of what harm could come to me. And of course, it's all about *me* in those formative years. We are little beings with amoeba-like fingers, just taking everything in - from swear words, to the tone of a voice, to the raising of a hand, to the softness of a parent's loving touch or a whisper. It is all assimilated so perfectly within us at such a young age. The trouble is whatever influences us then stays with us for a very long time in our lives and sometimes we are never able to uncover it. We become adults, busy with our lives, thinking we are healthy thriving successful human beings who have been perfectly nurtured and molded into who we are today.

Then when something suddenly goes awry in our relationships or blows up in our face, whether personal or professional, we wonder what the hell happened! What a shock! If we had been in touch with our little inner child experiences all along, there would be no surprises! But this is how so often our journeys and individual paths unfold, because of our unawareness of who we are, how and why we got here, and when we were shaped. What events played crucial roles in our lives? It is a bit of a catharsis, for it is this thirst to quench our purpose that is our very quest to exist!

We are born innocent, meant to play. Children play. I never did. Play is done without conscience, without worry, without threat or even thought. It just happens. It is spontaneous and most synonymous to just being. That, my friends, is what we are meant to be - human "beings".

Mr. A was an extension of my father - one more dysfunctional human being in a dysfunctional society that I now realize was hurt and shamed by *his* parents. Funny how I trusted him back then. As children, we do. In fact, we know nothing but trust. When we are born innocent - so perfect - the world is perfect - so true and good and honest and complete. And we are not jaded or hurt but instead, we are safe, or so we want to believe. Everything is always alright. We are always all okay and everyone and everything is so pure and all okay. Until.....a child's story begins.

My *real* dad was an alcoholic, a codependent if there ever was one. He would run away from problems, escape through his drinking and even when I tried to reconnect with him in my adult years, he turned me away. Story of my life! Abandonment is what I learned from the early age of two, when my parents divorced. It became the norm to be abandoned by anyone who I thought ever loved me, especially the men in my life, even as a young child, experiencing my mother's experiences with men. All I ever wanted so badly as a little girl growing up was a mom and a dad. They didn't have to be perfect - just a mom to love me and a dad to be there now and again. For these things I already knew intuitively at such a young age would make me whole, perhaps more complete.

Instead, I quickly learned to fear men and more predominantly my own identity. Mr. A's presence brought shame and fear, and although I was somehow saved by some miraculous universal karmic occurrence and my innocence was spared, he carved so much shame and guilt, fear and anxiety into my very being. This I have carried with me into my present existence.

Of course, along with all of this, a therapist would say goes low self-worth and self-esteem, issues of co-dependence, and most obviously, the inability to even know what a healthy male/female relationship should be like.

A lost soul, I have been lucky to find love, especially in my male relationships. Although my childhood was little else than walking on eggshells, I do still remember times of joy and safety. Where there is darkness, there is light. Where there is despair, there is hope. Where there is fear, pain, anger and anguish, there is love.

Life is about realizing that this is not about ever 'being there', but only how we get there. The other day I hiked for two hours to get to the 'grand waterfall' that everyone advised me to go see. When I arrived at the end of my journey, the waterfall was out of reach, only visible to the eye. I couldn't touch it. As beautiful and majestic as it was, I realized in that moment that it wasn't about the waterfall.

It was really the sun-enveloped two hour sea-breeze hike that had motivated me. The waterfall was only the excuse for going! It is simply what most would call the 'journey'. Take it for what it is and pray upon it. Feel the desperation, the fear, the pain, and through it all, the sun will shine to lighten the next day, just as it did the day before and the one before that. Meditate upon this if you have nothing else, for it will carry you from moment to moment, day to day, week to week, year to year. Life is all about ups and downs. Remember that it is a process, not an outcome. Enjoy the process, with all of its anguishes, disappointments and highs. The moment you are able to embrace it all is when you will be at peace with the realization that everything will be okay, just as you believed in your childhood innocence. And you believed right!

Life is a Playground!

So here I was, all alone for the first time in my life! How could I have let that be? I had just had my fortieth birthday and I was alone for the first time ever? I felt alive, somehow different, getting to know myself, finally! What had I been waiting for?

I love animals! They are great reminders of priority. Today, I was so completely completed with a renewed joy of watching and then participating in dog play upon miles and miles of white sandy beach. I was on the Washington Coast. I had decided that I was finally going to do it! Yes, I would take off on my own in my little jeep tracker to a place known to many to have the largest and most beautiful beaches in all of America. I simply had landed myself in the great State of Washington!

So away I went. It was the tail end of summer and into September. My little tracker was new to me. I had never taken it on a road trip and it had been sucking oil and sounding "funny" for weeks. But it was a fun little vehicle, very becoming of me and my personality at this stage in my life. When I purchased it as a straight across trade for my Jeep Cherokee, the ultimate gas guzzler, the guys in the lot shouted out to me as I playfully drove off, "That vehicle becomes you!" And it was! Free, simple and easy. I particularly loved the fact that I could take the top off (hers, not mine) and roll back the canvas to feel the sun and wind on my face, in my hair and all over my spirit! So after having the exhaust system rust out completely and having it replaced, I headed off, I must admit, with a little hesitation, but still fully committed.

The weather was perfect. In fact, everything was so perfect - not what I had expected, of course. I quickly learned after the first day of making point A to B safe and sound and still able to go the speed limit that I and this trip were going to be just fine! I could trust, relax, and enjoy without hesitation. I quickly realized that what I needed for so long had been too often lured away from me in my life by circumstance, people, love, obligation, commitment and distraction. Somehow I felt free for the first time in my life! Everything just fell so simply and so gracefully into place: The timing, the sunsets, the music on my drive, the flow of traffic, the relaxed state of being, and just knowing that I was exactly where I needed to be.

And where I was, on some beach somewhere, really did not matter. Nor did it matter what the clock said. I was simply immersed in the concept of play. Once again, the realization came to me that I had never really played or learned to play as a child. There were always conditions. I had two older sisters whom I depended upon dearly to be my playmates and my examples.

"Molly", they would say, "if you clean up, then we will play with you. If you do the supper dishes later, then we will play for half an hour more with you." If....then. If....then. As a result, I quickly learned that play meant conditions.

Today, in this moment, this was not the case! As my eyes filled up with overwhelming tears of joy, I relaxed into the very moment. There was no one, simply no one there to squash my desires or interrupt and judge my moment-to-moment thoughts. There was no one to tell me not to dance and no one to fear, no one to expect home any moment to ruin my fun. It was simple and pure, just as when we are born. As I watched the pups and birds and people frolic and run and chase Frisbees and squawk and fly and leap and bound, my inner self's cup filled up with love. And I was on my way!

I no sooner found myself with my pant legs rolled up, knee-deep in the beautiful playful waves of the omniscient ocean, and in that moment, nothing else mattered! I was immersed in joy, love and contentment. Everything we are born into this world with as children is there always just within arm's reach for us to grab hold of. The moment of realization was magical! Suddenly I clearly knew that my spirit had come alive and the realization hit me: *Play and spirit are one in the same!*

The rest of the day was simply magical! Everything just seemed to flow, like a babbling brook flowing from a river coming from a mountain top or from the ocean. Where it originated mattered not. It was just that the flow was natural and always present, determined and strong-willed, but still gentle.

And I played that whole four days, all by myself! I was so proud! I met so many people but without seeking the meetings, the attractions just happened! It was just as though the free spirits that would connect in those moments in time would come together in some magical way. There was no need for effort.

So how does one maintain this playful spirit? We are all born innocent, whole and perfect. When we 'grow up', most of us forget the word play. As adults out of necessity we are led to believe that we need to stop all that nonsense! Financial worries, insecurities with pensions and future retirement funds, emphasis on careers, looking successful to others and being busy all the time become our priorities and our lives. Now where really is the nonsense?

Just take a moment some time to sit and watch others at play. Observe the curl on their lips, the spunk in their run, the spring in their steps, the softness in their eyes. One need only look at children and animals, their obvious innocence and the fun they are having in their absoluteness and lack of ego. They are living in the moment, void of illusion of the past or expectations of what is to come in the future. We adults could take some lessons!

Stop and think for a moment about our concept of marriage. I would question whether it takes away from who we were really meant to be in spirit. Marriage grows us up, so to speak, and depletes our natural inner child tendencies. As a result, we are constantly bombarded with fear and disgrace should we dare show our little child side, especially once we have tied the knot. It is not mature, responsible, or acceptable. It's no wonder play is all too often halted in relationships as they denote yet one more grown up stage of dependency, enmeshment, security, stability, worry about the other person and ultimately a loss of memory for play.

In marriage, we become owners and keepers of the other. In essence, we capture and leash the spirit like capture of a wild animal that essentially thwarts the spirit and suffocates the soul, smothering the other in our so-called love. As a result, jealousy, possessiveness and all those illusionary human emotions can pervade the union and even prevent individual growth.

As I pondered all of this while sitting on the warm September sand, I asked the universe to reveal to me, "What really is love all about?" If it eventually leads to selfish ego boosting experiences in the human being, then how can this be love? Immediately, a universal voice was there. The waves spoke in volumes to me in that moment.

"Molly, you are so young as a spirit living a human experience. You have much to learn", the gentle waves spoke out in unison.

Then a flash of the past swept over me as I remembered back to when my sweet husband at the time, Jee, and I had taken a year sabbatical to play. We were sailing, green as could be, but we were doing it! Yes, living in the moment! And I could recall these moments of when we were happiest. It wasn't when we were in our most comfortable places with our possessions all around us, nor was it even necessarily when we were together.

Then a vision came to me so clearly. I could see Jee just as a little boy out in our humble little dinghy boat, bare backed to soak up the warm rays of the Florida sun. With fishing rod in hand all the while, he had not a care in the world if a fish was caught. All I could see from a distance at dockside was a faint outline of a sombrero hat to shade his fair-skinned face and head and the rest was like an aura - a wave of happy energy! He was in the moment and I could see clearly his spirit in full view. He was at play!

For me, play often involved enveloping myself in the local organic markets at various anchorages and seaside communities and townships along the way. It's people's efforts and energy to build something fun and beautiful yet profitable - a way of making ends meet - that has always been quite amazing to me! These people, simple as they might seem, have managed to understand and live the concept of making their work their play.

But even with all the stimulation brought on by newness of colors, markets, people, clothing, arts, crafts, and lively music to complete the scene, I can recall some of my best play moments were when we were at anchor and I was in solitude. Jee would escape the boat in the dinghy and go for a bike ride on land. Thinking back, it was probably those times that I treasured most. I loved the solitude, especially upon knowing that on the other side I had a wonderful relationship to fall back on. The one fear that often holds so many people back – loneliness - never entered my thoughts. I could play on the boat, fantasizing about being stranded and having to survive the last of the Titanic! How would I ever live? I loved the challenge of the moment! And what of the ocean's sand beaches? Some "hero" would sweep me away from the unbearable heat just before I would pass out. Oh how the irony of the hot sun and warm grains of sand mirrored the chains of agony of love, a love too much to handle at times. Jee always wondered how I never got soaked in boredom on those days when he needed to disembark from our safe little sailboat home on the water.

Sitting and pondering, I had to ask myself now, "What makes us as human beings happy?" Do animals even know the word - in fact, do children? For instance, why are so many of us animal lovers? Perhaps it is because we enjoy watching them in all their glory, naturalness, perfection and wholeness. Instinct, innocence and even intuition denote an element of play that sets the tone to their very existence.

And what about people who love children? Why do so many of us want to be around them? Is it because they are a procreation of us, of our own egos, our own existence, or because they will irrevocably carry on the next generation? What for? So why is this so significant? To better the world? To right all wrongs? To create a better future? Or perhaps to pay back some sort of karmic debt? The list can go on with all sorts of human thoughts of futuristic, optimistic perfectionism and idioms. It's all so intellectual and wise. I simply don't think it is that complicated. Children are simply an important link to remembering how to play!

Can't we just chalk it up to the simplicity of *play*, of knowing the child within ourselves? Do we, as human beings, always have to complicate life with so much analytical thought?

Have you ever noticed the way a puppy or kitten can only exist in the moment, the moment that is upon them right now? They have no other capacity, no other way of being. And the next moment comes and then they are in *that* moment, somehow transported magically there. They never feel sorry for themselves or get all caught up in worry. They may have fear at times, but only when the moment warrants fear. Somehow we believe we are different. Are we all that sad and out of touch that we have forgotten our true and beautiful innateness?

And the ocean spoke to me,

"Please listen to that tiny voice inside of you, Molly…for it speaks to you. It is always there. Go off and be alone somewhere and you shall hear it. Pay no mind to the little guy by the name of Doubt for he is there too. Alas, but so is your good friend, Faith. Listen to Faith. If you just practice hearing Faith, you will soon come upon your sneaky little friend named Ego who will most slyly lead you to your innermost self and introduce you to the beautiful I Am. If you are on top of your game, and once you know who I Am truly is, Ego will magically bow down because he will know that he cannot be defeated. Lo and behold you will eventually stumble upon an otherwise seemingly unattainable friend that's out there just beyond reach. Her name is Happiness!"

If you are now totally confused, just ask yourself one question: Do animals have ego?

Someone once told me that happiness is inherent in all of us, a God given right. As Dan Millman phrases it in his book, Way of the Peaceful Warrior,

"Now I realize that I had, in a sense, been sleeping all those years and just dreaming I was awake....I'd always believed that a life of quality, enjoyment and wisdom were my human birthright and would be automatically bestowed upon me as time passed. I never suspected that I would have to learn how to live."

I hear a voice, whispering and reminding me so reassuringly.

"Molly, remember that you are lovable, beautiful, whole and perfect, just as sure as the universe is pure and unfolding. Believe it or not," as the voice gets louder, "faith with understanding allows evolution in all of its magic and wonder. Clarity will just be there for you. There will be an immediate vision of a higher purpose in play."

How can it be that simple? Have you ever watched the ocean for more than a few minutes, or a seagull watching the ocean? Have you ever just sat and absorbed yourself in the wholeness of it all, simply to *become* part of it? When you *become* part of it, you just know instinctively how it feels in the dance, and you begin to understand the waves' propensity for play. Only then do you know that when you walk away and say good bye, you are only saying good night until tomorrow. For some reason you are so sure that those big dancing waves will be there, relentlessly bouncing, dancing, playing! But how do you know? How can you be so sure of the waves when you're not even sure about what will be there tomorrow in your own existence? Who will *you* be? What is *your* purpose? Where am *I* going? What is *my* perfect direction? You will become just as sure as you know the ocean will be there tomorrow when you *become* the ocean in all of its splendor, silence and recklessness!

In all the fifteen years of my married relationship, twelve years of which I was actually married, I can recall that the best years were in the beginning, when we both knew how to play so naturally without a moment's thought. About half way through our time together something snapped! The passion died and the magic faded. Is this what marriage holds? Some would simply accept this fate.

I quickly realized that our lack of passion in our relationship was spilling over into every pervading area of our lives - from work, to family, to play. Even the way we thought lacked passion. There was no longer a little life spark.

If you have never been there, where I am going, then think of this: Everyone can anticipate a vacation with pleasure even if only once a year. So why do we all look forward to and plan a vacation? Maybe it's simply because vacation time means play time! Think about it. When we go on vacation, we leave behind all worries and responsibilities. We reassure ourselves that we can forget and always catch up when we return. And that is how we live, with a break from what we believe to be the real world. But, in fact, the real world *is* our vacation!

Some say that life is an illusion. It is only when we let go of worry, fear and anxiety for what we think is to come in our future that we can begin to relax into our own comfort, our own play zone, our own inner child, our own love for ourselves and what we really deserve - physically, mentally, emotionally and spiritually. This is when we can tap into our higher selves – our *real* selves. And it is then that we begin to know how much we really belong to the universe and how much we *are* the universe!

So what's a holiday worth to anyone? A holiday is play time! It's when we can let go of worry, which by the way, is completely an illusionary emotion of no value, not even to motivate, believe it or not.

Unfortunately, most of us never get to this stage in our fast paced lives. Besides that, we are termed as 'lazy' if we are not living in a so-called successful world of phones ringing and arriving home at all hours, dining out for lunch daily and wining and dining by night in a corporate world.

So why do we continue to punish ourselves? "Why can't my life be fun, easy, simple?" we ask. We want it all. That's why. Most of us can't even remember what if feels like to have passion, or we never felt it in the first place. We never got that far before the sad reality of becoming adults set in.

Elation on Fire! Grief Consuming

Oh my good God and Universal Wisdom – give me some clarity! Why do sad things have to happen in order to see clearly and feel happy? Why must we human beings feel grief, sadness and sorrow before we can experience joy, elation, highs and lows?

Intimacy is set apart from space and coldness. Yes, we all construct our own walls of coping and as a result, we often push those we love most away. In particular, I can recall living much of my life in relationships this way.

When Jee and I met we were hot for each other! I was in a relationship that was, let's just say, emotionally compromising. Surprise, surprise! Even scarier was the fact that I had a big fat ring on my finger! Eager to tie the knot and probably go on to have children with a 'boy' I had been infatuated with since leaping out of the safety and confines of my childhood home, I was on the verge and really very desperate to escape my misery, yet unable to really completely face it. Lacking self-esteem, I was confused and unsure of where to go next.

Then Jee came along. His energy and wisdom carried me away from the stark reality of the boy I was almost ready to commit my whole life to! Jee was different from anyone, any male I had ever experienced in all of my growing pains at home. For one thing, he was eighteen years my senior, which should have alerted me to a need for someone to be in my life that I had otherwise lacked as a true father figure.

But I was twenty-three and fumbling through life, just doing my best and struggling along.

There is *a reason, a season and a lifetime* for everyone who preciously comes into your life. For instance, has the thought ever occurred to you that you may have more than one soul mate in a lifetime, or that you possibly may not have any control over who enters your life? These souls come onto your path almost as if they were special earth angels, the ones necessary to help you along at various stages of your life, to help you learn lessons. Perhaps that script was pre-written.

When we can accept that we only have limited control over the atrocities of life, the unfairness, unfortunate occurrences and the suffering and wrong-doings that are supposedly done to us and the rest of the world, when we can accept this as *what is,* this is when we can truly become free of resentment, anger and hatred and allow room for love and acceptance to ultimately grow from our experiences. Believe it or not, not everything in life works out exactly the way we may think it should. How very egotistical to even imply that, don't you think? How dare we think we have that much control or wisdom over evolution, when we are no more than mere ants on a sidewalk within a city of sidewalks? That's where we don't get it. The 'wrongness' is not in the way things evolve, but in our unrealistic expectations of them and the perceived control that we think we have over all of it.

Do you ever feel elated in one moment and hope that feeling never goes away? But sure as the stars are in the sky, it always does and then a feeling such as grief replaces it. They are complete polar opposites. For you to experience one, you must endure or enjoy the other. That's because both feelings are actually a part of one in the same! We are lucky that the universe leaves the experience up to us!

Estrangement

I am homeless again! I was homeless for a short time when I mustered up the courage to leave the contentment and sureness of my life, a world of stability and security. Although I was uprooting what had become a gray world, it was still scary.

So here I was. Yes, you could find me easily those days. I was the one with the little pink knit cap wandering around the downtown streets of a sleepless little city.

I said good bye once more to my humble safe haven, the cottage at land's end of the island I was living on at the time. As I glanced around the tiny suite that had once been a garage now converted into a cozy unique living space with character, I thanked the space once filled with aromatic smells of sage sticks and burning essential oils, warm brown rice and herbs, and the simplicity and safety that it offered me in a time of need. This little space had housed me for six months, protecting me from the mayhem of the outside world. And I was giving it up now.

Where would I go? I felt estranged and unsettled yet excited all at once! It is not until we become uprooted that we begin to realize our limits, our balance and our *real non-illusionary* needs. Living in a surreal world is not what most seek to discover. I, on the other hand, was on a journey of a gypsy, a butterfly, into somewhat of the unknown. I liked the thoughts of that, as scary as it seemed.

My stomach churned and my head ached for days. For I was letting go of the known, the comfortable life and the cushioning I had been provided over the past six months. But I knew deep within that a greater force was pushing me to discover my greater purpose. And that excited me!

In the meantime, I had had a very special angel enter my life. Not knowing for sure what his purpose would be, I trusted him. He had helped me seek shelter when I uprooted my life the first time and found a neat little bus converted to living space. I loved it! It was free and fun and easy. But eventually I longed for more – perhaps a home with a few things I could call mine. I wasn't really sure. But I did have some very definite visions as to how I could see myself living to most benefit my character in this stage of my life, and make me a better person in the process.

I wanted a wood burning stove, a natural way to keep warm over our damp bone chilling island winters. And I wanted the place to be completely imperfect! I wanted flaws and imperfections. I wanted not what I had sought in my recent past. Perhaps it was because I was going through a period of rediscovery, a somewhat reckless stage, finding Molly again. It was a whole new side that I had never had a chance to know.

I wanted to grow my hair and wear it in the dreaded dreadlocks! I wanted to smoke weed and feel funny and numb and hallucinatory and whatever else weed is supposed to do! I wanted to laugh out loud, scream and cry. I wanted to run past dark until I was lost and too tired to go any further. I wanted to simply let go!

My life had been so damned perfect up until now! In fact, Jee used to boast about our most perfect relationship, how we never argued, how he had the most perfect wife, the most perfect communication, even the perfect cat! Frankly, that's ultimately what drove me away. It simply took away the fire! I always desired to share my imperfections and struggles with those around me and often I felt tied to bonds that wouldn't allow for it. It would be too devastating for the image. Well, to hell with image! I never wanted it in the first place! Who was I trying to impress, if not myself?

So here I sat, one year later, after twelve pretty great years of marriage, disillusioned with relief. One thing I have learned for certain - there is never forever in life nor are there any guarantees. We, as human beings, are ever changing, just as is the universe as it continues to evolve and unfold, all the more reason to enjoy the moment and leave worry behind. There is no past and no future. It is only the moment that is real. We so often fail to realize that there is always an element of destiny in our outcomes, much easier stated than understood.

Without destiny, the unknown, and that which we cannot control, the definition of humankind would most certainly be different. But that is not for us to say, nor is it our role or our purpose here on Earth. Otherwise our collective name would be Universe, or even God! We, as human beings, do have the ability to tap into that divine light to contribute to the good will of the universe. Now that is divine purpose! And that is what is exciting and amazing! Lucky us to be given such a gift, don't you think?

At the same time, we must realize and accept those things we cannot change and move forward with those tasks that we are capable of in our everyday lives. These are gifts we have been given. We need to acknowledge them and use them wisely. Dr. Wayne Dyer speaks of the light within each and every one of us and notes that "if you go through life looking for imperfections, focusing on what's wrong, focusing on what's missing, focusing on what you can't have, you are not living from the light…and…if you really want to understand living from the light and understand living without dichotomies and without opposites…try to imagine…a house on the sun…Would there be such a concept for you as darkness?"

But what about when things don't go the way we wanted, when life is all wrong and the universe decides to throw us a curve ball? These too are gifts of lessons to be learned in order to ultimately contribute to the healing of the earth. These experiences are there to help us pave the way to our next life in the physical as we know it, and to ultimately transcend beyond the physical into spirit.

The Angels Are Back!

Recognize them when they come into your life. Be in tune, ready and open to accept them because they will not be there forever, most times only fleeting, to see if you are ready for them to help you, as if they are playfully testing your awareness of them. There are definite signs of angels in everyone's lives. The key is being perceptive enough to recognize them when they come, for most often, they surface when you are least expecting them!

Angels come in and out of our lives for very good reasons. They are there to help us learn our lessons and to contribute to our growth. They allow us to do the work, but they take our hands during special journeys and missions to help us accomplish what we came here to do in any given lifetime. They give us hope and inspire us to keep going.

I will readily admit that one such angel in my life was my husband at the time. Now divorced, I can most candidly confess that he was an angelic force in the last fifteen years of my life while with him. He rescued me from an almost mistake of a marriage and from the dooms of my dark and dingy basement suite at the time. He taught me much about spirituality, wisdom and love. He even provided for me financially and held so much compassion for all life. We had a companionship that was like no other. He literally took me on a short cut to learning. I acknowledge his love and I have undying gratitude for having had him in my life in such a strong capacity during those years.

Another very important angel in my life was Cacao the Champagne Cat. He was that amazing pink color with a bubbly, funny personality that could make anyone laugh! Cacao and Jee were simultaneous angels that had come into my life for a reason together. Looking back now, I realize that their symbiotic existence in my world was certainly not by chance.

The Wonder Cat

I had had many cats in my childhood. We would always just naturally adopt them as strays. They just seemed to know through their own incredible intuition where they would find refuge. They would usually be outdoor/indoor kitties, so more often than not, we would lose them to being hit by a car or they would just go missing. We always cried when we lost one, but never like the mourning and grieving that Jee and I experienced when our dear Cacao exited this world. That's when I realized how different and special he was. He had been there as an angel to both of us until he was no longer needed and his mission was complete.

Cacao was a hero in his own right. He was more simply a wonder cat with a short lived life and a long 'tail' of miraculous teachings never to be forgotten, one sure sign of a true angel. He was so beautiful, so innocent and a definite show off! The thing that I can remember most about him when I first set eyes on him is that he was looking for someone to love him. As we walked into the local pet store of the third world town we had decided to call home until hurricane season was over, we were not anticipating what we might find.

Jee and I were in the midst of volunteering for a local spay and neuter project that was spearheaded by an American couple who traveled the world giving their time and efforts for animal relief. We had just finished our own quest of sailing across open seas and were 'green' from having lived and grown up in the mountains and prairies. The sail itself would be one nerve racking adventure! But we made it, and now it was time to delve into our real passions. It was time to reach out and help these people with the rescue and treatment of animals in need of care here.

It was crazy and sad. The street dogs in the Caribbean were called pot cakes because the only food they had access to was what locals would give them from the bottom of their cook pots from the night before dinner or morning breakfast. These dogs were wild and they quickly learned to catch and kill as their means of survival. Sadly, many street felines fell prey to their jaws. One morning when volunteering for the local vet working with the spay/neuter project, we discovered a dead cat at the door. She had made her last ditch plea for help in the midst of the morning dew, but we were too late.

Many of the animals we took in were so infested with fleas and ticks that the creepy little crawlers had grown so large and swollen from enjoying a never ending stream of blood from their prey. We could just pull them off like balls of blisters. The dogs especially participated with courage, for they seemed to know we were helping them. One cat came in so chilled that we had to keep a blow dryer on her to keep her body temperature up. All in the heat of the tropics, she was a survivor!

We eagerly assisted in spay and neuter surgeries as well. Although we had no formal education, our hands were welcomed with enthusiasm. The most difficult part of it was dealing with the emotion of it all. Oh how I wanted so much to tell the dogs and cats what was happening to them so that they would feel no fear and everything would be just fine when they would awake. Sometimes it was a little scary as it seemed the anesthetic didn't fully take effect. We would be half into the surgical procedure and the animal would flinch and move! Dr. H assured us it was alright and that they couldn't feel anything.

Somehow our fate met with a sweet little kitten's fate one day during all of this. I do believe all of the experiences and moments with the animals demanding so little of us gave us even more compassion when we walked into the pet store that day.

What happened next was amazing! I walked right past the little furry spectacle to a tiny sweet helpless black kitten someone had named Mary.

"Let's take this little sweetie home, Jee!" I exclaimed.

Of course, we hadn't strolled into the store to come out with anything less than an experience! But what the hell was happening? Although Jee's attention was momentarily drawn to my exclamation, he quickly redirected me to the little pinkish blonde tabby making a spectacle of himself in his tiny home, a little cage of bars.

"Look at this, Mol!" he exclaimed. "This little guy is doing summersaults to attract our attention!"

My gaze quickly went to Jee's intrigue. We laughed and felt sorry for the little guy all at the same time. How did he end up in here? I had to hand it to him, as he sure was making the best of his situation in the moment. He was making a spectacle of himself and with purpose! It was as if he knew he needed to look somehow different from all the rest of the lovable creatures in the store so that we would notice him most.

She was a stout young Bahamian woman caring for the animals by day and heading home to abandon them by night. After all, she had a family of her own to tend to. And this, well it was only a job.

We returned the next day once again even more intrigued by the little champagne-colored feline. This time we asked Teresa if we could hold him. We wanted to see just how eager he was to find a new home. Wow! He was a bomb shell! Although he was obviously in his own little nirvana to have all the space in the store to roam, he stuck close to me as I held him and he seemed to enjoy continually nibbling on my wedding ring, as if to say, "That's some bond you two got going there!" As he curiously explored all the store's counter tops, walls and floors, we had to contain him so as not to lose him to the ceiling! He was a handful but a most lovable one at that. Our hearts were already too far gone as we were attached with tight strings instantaneously. Oh no! What did this mean?

I had had cats in my childhood, but Jee never had. I knew that this one would prove to be a lifetime experience for him. He had no clue what he was in for but he could see the look of love and compassion in my eyes for this little creature that was so desperately seeking love. Now he knew there was no turning back. We figured the rest of his litter mates had been adopted out and he was the "Last of the Mohicans", the odd one out. We knew what that was like as we had both been there in our own walks of life - in our own families, in the world in general, feeling many times like we didn't belong.

We didn't make a decision in that moment, for that was not Jee's way and I respected that. If it had just been me, the spontaneous one, that cat would have been out the door in that very second! But besides that, we had not the means to transport him back to our humble abode aboard our sailboat. It was a Saturday as the store was closing and we had to leave the little guy back in his small home of bars. We were solemn and sad.

On Sunday, we returned to the store on our trusty little vehicles, our old faded folding bikes which we had carried across the ocean with us. They were great friends to us. We had provisioned our entire boat before sailing to the Bahamian waters via our cycling vehicles. We had stocked ourselves with canned goods, bottles of wine, vacuum cleaners, bedding, dishes and all kinds of sundries that would prepare us for our voyage on these bikes alone. Well, now we were back on our bikes to retrieve this little life form that so intrigued us and had so quickly stolen our hearts.

Much to our disappointment, the store was closed. As we pushed our noses against the thin glass-paned windows, we were sorry we hadn't snafued the little guy right there and then the day before. He seemed to sense our presence as we cupped our hands to peer at him through the hot tropical weathered windows from outside. We could hear him meowing and crying for us as if to say, "Please come and get me. I will be sure to make you happy, and teach you a lesson or two, I promise!"

Although the area could accommodate a variety of tourists and well-to-do people with sailboats as one of their many commodities, it was very much a third world type of community, meaning nothing in the way of frills. Everything worth eating or buying was at least eighteen times more than what we ever had in our not so expandable pockets. We felt our plates were full so we naturally questioned giving a cat a good life. I know it wasn't like having a child but we still had our doubts.

We decided that day after seeing him cry out that we would return first thing Monday morning to retrieve him. As humble as we felt, we thought we could offer him a more promising life on a sailboat than a cage could. We would introduce him to a whole new world, a world different from that of any other cat, possibly not the best world for a cat – a mere sailboat? But he would prove to offer us more than any other cat in return. Little did we know how true that would be!

We had rigged a milk crate to the back of Jee's bike with a lid of screen and cardboard box. Monday morning could not come soon enough. We were excited to be off to pick up our little package!

Butter

We called him Cacao. He was the color of butter, only sweeter, like a sweet thick Liquor of Crème de Cacao. We could have called him Pink Champagne as that was his true color, but in the spirit of the Bahamas we decided that "Cacao" was a great combination of the cays (pronounced keeys) and the color of the well-known liquer. Hence, he came by his name quite honestly. We quickly became accustomed to calling out his name in a rhythmic song-like fashion.

We somehow managed to sloppily get the sweet little pink furry creature back to our humble abode that day to board our home. Our twenty-nine foot live-aboard sailboat that we called home would now be home to Cacao too. From that moment on the little guy had hold of our hearts in a big way!

He was the epitome of playfulness and happiness in the moment, and he instantly brought much joy into our lives. As we plucked the tiny creature from his temporary middle class transportation unit made of soggy salty-aired cardboard, he truly exhibited the most curious and grateful personality that amazed and amused us both. He was free from what he knew to be his home, a tiny cage constricting his movement behind metal bars, and it was as if he was celebrating his new found freedom. After all, a huge spirit cannot exist forever in confinement! He was a true master of living in the moment. As I stopped to admire his natural qualities, something about me envied him, and I knew at that moment, that I was about to embark on a journey of play with Cacao as a constant reminder of my priorities in life – adventure, risk, play, excitement, living in the moment, anticipation and love.

Living on a boat, everything was unrefrigerated, so whatever was left out was suddenly a topic of curiosity by our new little friend. I can still remember so clearly the picture in my mind. Jee was videoing our new arrival. All at once he would disappear and then his tiny pink head would pop up and reappear from somewhere. Even in the midst of our tiny boat, he would find a place to blend in and lose himself. He was so small himself, probably a mere six weeks old. His little life seemed so insignificant to the locals but oh so magical to us. His playful spirit never ceased to amaze us! We would frequently find ourselves absorbed in play right along with him, and in the moment. Suddenly his little head with rather large disproportionate ears were hard to miss. Up he popped from the galley sink and took a nose dive straight into the butter dish! The creamy texture of the pale yellow butter soaked itself into his tiny furry face as he smacked his lips in surprise and pleasure.

Chaos!

"He will be strictly a boat cat!" we exclaimed (as if we had any say in the matter). For anyone who knows anything about cats knows that *they* rule, we don't dictate!

From the very first evening aboard, he was a true natural sailor cat. We had packed him up and couriered him over to have an inaugural sundowner with our buddy boat friends who were moored across the bay. They, by the way, were the ones who ultimately convinced us to adopt Cacao. Now they wanted to be formally introduced. So off the three of us motored in our little inflatable dinghy. Cacao, having no fear of the ride, the water, the motor, the noise or the newness of it all, reminded me of me! Eager to explore and poised for the unknown, off we went.

And so on went his little life, absolutely as important as ours was! He would lounge on the mast, bask in the sun on the foredeck at every anchorage and stretch out on the sole of the sailboat awaiting our return from a day of chores or pleasures on shore. Of course, the first thing we would always anticipate eagerly upon returning on our dinghy would be his furry little body. We would see who could spot him first. It became a game.

He added so much fun, purpose and laughter to our lives at a time that could have otherwise been very worrisome and depressing. We had socked all our investments into the markets and they had disappointed us sorely. The markets had tumbled and we were left to wonder how we might survive on our plan.

How *would* we survive with no money coming in - no way of making a living? We were surviving all right, with the help of our little friend, Cacao! He would follow us endlessly down forbidden trails through the thick of the forest. People would ask us, "Is that a cat or a dog?" and "How did you train him to do that?" The intriguing part was that he was never on a leash! In fact, we never taught him anything of the sort. He just simply chose to stay with us because we freely gave him that choice, I guess.

At one particular anchorage, Cacao and I made a pact. If he would not run away from me, I would take him for a harrowing ride across the water in the dinghy to the local park so he could feel the grass beneath his feet, smell the flowers and chortle the birds. For the most part, he stuck by his part of the pact but at times he was a typical cat and he would disappear on me for much longer than I cared for him to be out of my sight. During those times, he slowed me down and I found myself stopping to smell the flowers and feeling the grass beneath my own feet. The cat definitely had a way of creating play and pleasure and helping me to experience one in the same.

But even when we would do an all-night crossing, or when the winds and weather would get rough and unpredictable, Cacao stuck by us. He was calm and grounded, atypical of the usual skittish feline behavior in such conditions. He would lay beneath Jee's feet at the helm while underway in the shallow and often unsafe feeling cockpit. When the waves rocked, Cacao rocked with them. He never once showed fear. We grew to depend on him as our ocean crossing mascot. He made us laugh and life was light even in the midst of what otherwise looked like imminent disaster! When we would approach docking we would pop him into his kitty kennel until we were safely moored. He was always so good and never once struggled during these times. It was as if he knew exactly when and why it was happening. Smart cat!

He never complained, not while underway anyway. He just accepted his life as an atypical cat. He was always thankful for us and it seemed as if he could always remember sadder days when he was imprisoned and now life was good indeed! He was a cat who could always make the best of it all. The only times I can remember even a mere complaint was when we would try to sneak away on our bikes and he would cry out for us in a low pitched pitiful mow! We would try to quietly skulk out when he wasn't looking, like two children trying to get away with something real big. Oh how the guilt consumed us as we could hear him from miles away, and then he would fade.

Cacao was not without challenge for us. In fact, he liked to test us from time to time just to see how much we really cared, or maybe just to see what he could get away with. One night, we found ourselves on a rooftop at a house party trying to rescue him. There were wild pot cakes all around and he was no fool. He wasn't coming down for nothing!

After what seemed like hours that had passed, that night Cacao finally learned to trust my loving arms as they reached out to pluck him to safety, and sleep at last! He had grown too tired to stay atop the roof and didn't want to spend the night alone. He seemed to know we would eventually give up on him, deserting him and leaving him to come down on his own. So in desperation, he finally outstretched his arms to sink his tiny pink paws into my fleshy, warm shoulders. Jee was behind me all the way to catch us both if we should come crashing down. That night was the beginning of a whole new trust between us.

There were so many such so-called rescues that Cacao invited. One night, while moored at a popular beach marina, we were white with fright by what we saw! We had been out having sushi with some friends who had been visiting from Canada. We had taken the bus home to our sailboat abode ready to bunk down after a fun night out. Ritualistically, we climbed on board to our usually dedicated welcoming committee named Cacao. But tonight felt different. Ever since we had docked at this busy marina, we were always fearfully anticipatory of coming home to an empty boat. Instinctively, we knew something was very wrong. As we climbed down the companionway, we both had an eerie feeling. Tonight there was no Cacao!

The current in the bay was deadly enough to carry anything that fell prey to its demise away for good. We day sailed very little here because docking was so difficult due to the current. Naturally, we were extremely concerned when we arrived back at the boat and Cacao was nowhere to be found! Our hearts sank and the nausea of loss began to creep over us.

We were already going through the stark realization that this was it. All the sailings, rescues and adventurous times with our little Cacao would be no more. It was all over. Understand that this cat had already braved out more than his nine lives, having fallen in the waters numerous times, been chased by wild pot cakes and escaped by leaping into shark infested waters! He had even crossed the big black sea all night with us. And now....he was gone.

We would take one last look for him. It was always in my nature to never give up hope until it's time. I was always fearful that he would wander off onto the gambling boat at the end of the dock that did its nightly cruise and casino runs. As much as Cacao could have had his adventures and fun aboard The Gambler, this was certainly no place for a feline.

Side stepping the dock with flash light in hand, Jee and I scoured the waters, fearful of what we may or may not find. There were numerous times that the damn cat had fallen in only to grab hold of the barnacled dock post and yell his sorry fool head off until someone would rescue him. In fact, one day we returned home to a poor young lad who had plucked him off a dock post. The young man was literally bloodied with skid marks from head to toe from having to launch the clinging cat to safety. Bless that brave boy's compassionate heart!

But tonight would be different. There was no Cacao to be seen beneath the docks. Just as we were ready to give up and hope by some miracle that the cat would return on his own in the morning, I caught something out of the corner of my eye. In my peripheral vision and somewhat of a woman's instinct, I could almost smell the feline fur nearby. As I turned to my left, there he was! He was sitting calmly on the rear transom of a gorgeous 50-foot Halberg Rassey sailboat!

Smoothing over his wet coat with his rough pink tongue, he seemed rather unbothered by the fact that he had obviously just moments ago fallen into the rapids of the undying current beneath him. It was as though he had turned a blind eye to all and deserted us to live some other rich lifestyle! How dare he? At first, I was overwhelmed with relief. As I cried out to Jee to return from his search at the north end of the dock, I could feel the humor of it all envelope me. "One more life still left!" I thought, and I silently chuckled to myself in relief and disbelief.

We quickly concluded that he must have barely saved himself as he would have fallen in and somehow managed to overcome the strength of the current to grab onto the transom of one of the nicest sailing vessels in the whole marina. I had to conclude – the cat's got class!

From that moment on, Cacao continued to live a 'non- cat' existence. He was like no other feline living somewhat of an atypical life. Even once we moved off our sailboat to a more typical lifestyle, he always found a way to get into more trouble, and he was often even bored and somewhat restless with a land locked lifestyle. After all, *Chaos* had become his middle name. He certainly had no problem ever living up to it. In fact, he earned it!

Through all of it though, Cacao took us away from what otherwise would have been a very worrisome time in our lives. He had made us forget our worries by dissolving our stress and ultimately helping us to finish what we had started – a journey of play. Through Cacao we were able to live in the moment, and for that we will be forever grateful and indebted to him.

Lessons From a Divine Feline

When Cacao's fate was to leave us seven and a half years later, we were shocked and completely traumatized with the means of his departure.

It just wasn't fair. We always thought we knew he would be swept up and taken away by an owl or an eagle after a long and harrowing struggle, or that he just wouldn't return one night after an unsolved adventure into the darkness – lost perhaps, or food for the coyotes. Our imaginations went wild. We always thought that is how an adventurous cat *should* go.

Little did we know what would strike him so suddenly and out of the blue. No, it wasn't a wild animal, or a lost night in the woods with no return, and not even a fatal injury from a vicious fight in the wild.

It wasn't until almost one year after I had left our marriage – almost eight years after returning back to Canada having put our sailing adventures to rest – that Cacao's fate took hold and finally dissolved a chance at one more of the more than nine lives that he had lived. This time he had spent them all.

As we had never had children, Cacao was our little boy. He meant the world to us and was probably more child-like to us than anyone could ever possibly imagine or even begin to try to understand. With his passing there was insurmountable grief. Jee and I were forced to lean on one another, and for a time, the little feline's fate brought us closer together again.

Coincidently, we happened to be reconsidering our relationship at the time. We had discussed the possibility of making it work and perhaps going on a road trip some place for a year sabbatical to rediscover some passion, spark and magic. Perhaps we would buy a recreational vehicle and head somewhere remote and tropical, working on 'us' all the while.

But something changed all that. With Cacao's passing there was no longer anything binding us together. He had become our common thread for eight years. He was all we had left to share in the moment, other than our memories of lost adventures passed. Without Cacao we were lost. We dropped all contemplations to try again when we felt something different, empty and not right. Too much had happened and too much was gone now.

It wasn't until I got over the grief of losing Cacao months later, when I came to an amazing realization! Cacao's departure from the physical world had freed us to do what we both now needed to do more than ever, and that was to move on. That was becoming more and more clear.

That wonderful cat quickly acquired the name *'Divine Miracle Feline'* as he was recognized so clearly as having had 'a reason and a season' for having had come into both our lives. He knew absolutely more than both of us put together! He was courageous, forth giving, and purposeful to let go when he did.

He was a miracle and a lesson to us both that animals can simply live in the moment and go to the spirit world in the next. They come and they go when the timing is right and divine – all without hesitation and without expectation. There was no fear, only acceptance and love, just as I witnessed in Cacao's eyes the day he let go of his physical existence and soared into the spirit world.

Precious Emotional Connect

I left our marriage in the winter of 2006. We had had two miserable winters in a row on the island, which was very unusual for what is otherwise known as Canada's 'Little Hawaii'. The mild weather was one of the main driving forces that had brought us back to Canada after having lost so much financially in the stock market when we were sailing. Our plan had failed miserably and we were forced to return to Canada.

I can recall feeling blue and depressed for a long time leading up to my departure. Perhaps it was two years that had passed. I could never really put my finger on it, but I always thought I had never made the opportunity for myself to find my own way, create my own path, discover my unique direction and feel good about doing it all by myself. For some reason, I had written my script with someone always there to rescue me, someone to carry me, not only in times when my knees gave out and I couldn't walk, or when I fell down and couldn't get back up, but at all times. Even when I thought I was strong and capable, there was always someone there. Perhaps it was because there was never anyone there while I was growing up. Remember? Abandonment was my issue. There was never a father figure, something I had always yearned for as a child, more than anything. So maybe I learned how to over compensate at a very young age. I went from having no one to anyone who would have me.

Those are *my* issues though. I left because I needed to discover *me* once and for all! I was feeling smothered and foggy, and I wanted to break free and breathe it all in as it happened. I needed to take the chances and feel the highs and the lows on my own. There was really no other choice.

The week of my departure from our so-called *perfect* world and *perfect* marriage (and actually it was in many ways), I was so overwhelmed with desire. I had never seen myself so desperate, so needy of love and so fulfilled by another. I wanted so badly to *feel* again. I wanted to make the numbness disappear. I must admit I was completely selfish. The need to fulfill the higher levels of 'Maslow's Hierarchy of Needs' had become unavoidable. I suppose I had secretly denied myself of the inevitable and it was ultimately creating confusion for both of us.

As a result, I encouraged Jee to get out of town despite the bad weather and imminent storm. I had to do what I had to do. I didn't care where he went or what he did. All I knew in that moment was that I had to fill my own cup. I had to save myself. I had never felt so desperate for passion… and so selfish! In my desperation to fulfill my own needs, I selfishly sacrificed Jee's safety, and more compassionate thought and reasoning, to my own desires. One last ditch effort to rediscover our passion had proven so obviously absent that my convictions to send him away were reinforced even more without question. I knew in that very moment that our passion, our spark, our magic had died. I was soulfully sad and Jee had no clue.

He departed the next day in a bastardly snow storm. Even my own mother questioned my convictions. How could I send my husband, someone I loved, away in such conditions? What was I thinking? How bad of a person was I?

Up until my departure, I had not shared my desperation, my loneliness, my desires to search for more, with anyone. I always only admitted within the confines of our marriage that I wanted to 'work on' our passion next year. Well eventually next year was not soon enough. I wanted more than to work on it. I wanted passion *now.* I realized later that one doesn't *work on* passion. It's either there or it's not. And I had already discovered that it was wholly absent. Because I didn't share any of this with anyone, when I made the break, I literally caught everyone by surprise!

When I left, he chose not to see the signs of my misery and ultimately my intentions of never returning to our home, our relationship and our life together. When I look back, I don't think either of us yet believed it nor did we want to. It was too hurtful, and too terrifying. In fact, when I packed and headed off in my jeep a day after his return, I really was not sure what the outcome might be. I didn't know what a week or even a few days would bring as far as emotions were concerned. All that mattered was that moment.

But he prepared me with a map and a kiss good-bye, knowing that something was very wrong but choosing to allow me my freedom to discover what that was. The look in his eyes that day when he wished me a great trip, which must have taken a tremendous amount of courage and strength on his part, was a 'simple something' look that had been missing for us both. I could see then, in that moment, that he was dedicated and committed, and that he was not going to be the one to step outside of our comfort zone to risk our marriage. As I saw the lack of zest in his eyes that had been there for so long, I knew it was up to me to leap into a bed of courage and take that chance....for both of us. It was the only way to give us both a chance at finding our spirits again.

Intimacy or Into Me See?

When I forced Jee's departure before I actually left our relationship, it had stormed something fierce. I had had a chance to step into intimacy like I had never experienced in my life. The storm itself encouraged closeness, warmth and natural attraction.

He was from one of the smaller neighboring islands. I had met him very innocently at the ferry terminal when we were both embarking on new careers. He had just returned from India and was creating a new direction for himself with essential oils and amazing perfume creations.

I was embarking on a new career myself. I had just returned from California from completing my massage practitioner training and I was out to try some of my new found skills in a less intimate environment where I could make a quick buck doing chair massage for those people awaiting their ferries, looking for something to do, looking for touch.

To be truthful, I wasn't really enjoying what I was doing all that much. After all, chair massage wasn't my passion and certainly not the reason I had gone to school in the beautiful Big Sur, California region, with all of its magical energy abounding.

But when Jay came along, it was actually what *he* was doing that intrigued me most. He had gone from a very masculine life of building and contracting to a world of mystical feminine smells and therapeutic oil blends. He always joked with me later that he decided to make such a radical change so that he could find a woman who enjoyed touch - someone perhaps who was a massage therapist!

Although I was extremely inhibited in the beginning, I was also curious about what he was all about. As innocent as it was, he intrigued me. But I had no right to feel anything else. I was married! Still, I could not ignore his demeanor, his style, his uniqueness. He had a definite *island* look about him - you know, the *bare - foot – blue – jeans – long – hair - with pony – tail – free – spirited* - look! He was a little rough around the edges with a total masculinity surrounded by a sensitive side and a more feminine aura. There was something about that that drew me in. He would pop over to my booth to chat. We would eat our lunches together. I would practice my massage techniques on him and he would rub my feet with a new peppermint foot lotion he wanted to test. It was play in its most initial form. And it was nice.

When one of us would leave the scene early, a small shadow of disappointment would overcome the other. But when we were both present it was always so much fun to pass the time away on slower days and bee bop back and forth on busier ones. We exchanged business cards and nothing more developed.

Weeks went by. Then one day a most uplifting email came to me. He was simply sweet and genuine. He was merely sharing his feelings, innocently and without ego, admitting that he missed my sweet bright smile and ray of sunshine when I wasn't there. He would look over at that huge space all day, once filled with light and love and was now void of energy and presence. I was touched.

Well, needless to say, that started the ball rolling! No sooner did I find myself not quite stepping outside of my marriage, but wanting to get to know him, just a little better. I would email him with excuses to book a relaxation massage and he would playfully reply back with a new prescription he had concocted for me to help heal my clients. *"Molly's Very Own Deep Tissue Massage Cream made with love by Jay"* was a complete recipe for romance! Actually, it wasn't difficult to feel the love in all of his products and I didn't hesitate to let him know.

From then on, I would look forward to an evening alone when I could call Jay. He never called me as he correctly assumed I was probably in a relationship and respected that without question. Whenever I called I always assumed he probably had a few women in *his* life, as frequently women would answer the phone. I later discovered that sometimes it was his daughter and other times it was a good friend who was living and renting on his land or helping him make products. In any case, it never mattered. I expected nothing from him. Whenever I contacted him, I always received a listening ear and an opened mind.

We would chat on the phone for hours at a time getting to know each other more intimately with every call. Eventually we began to want more - perhaps a bike ride together one day, or a trip to the island to discover *his* world, or even a glass of wine or two just to exchange services and products.

Before I knew it, *I* was inviting *him* to dinner and a night out on the town with intentions of ending up in some romantic hotel room somewhere to explore each other to yet another level. I was excited by the moment once more.

Another Place in Time

Today I sat and watched the ocean. I was at its mercy. I had hiked alongside the shore thinking the whole time that the tide was falling. How could I have been so wrong? Actually, I was doubting myself the whole time, some sort of intuition perhaps. I had a strange feeling in my gut.

The tide was, in fact, *rising* and now there was no time for guess work! My feet, ankles and legs were being battered and tripped up by logs and garbage that had been strung alongside the beach from months of floating in from across the bay and collecting on the shoreline. I had heard that people had broken ankles and been washed out to sea in a panic due to such unexpected tidal behavior. The fear and panic set in!

Imagine you are out for a great hike along the beachside one day, anticipating the immediate future of a great dinner that night with your family, friends, partner and all those you love. Ah yes, you will have a sweet story to tell of your beautiful day, you think. But in the next unexpected moment, you are gone! The turns that life takes sometimes make one realize that we really never know when our time is up. This is how fragile life really is. At times we tread on water and almost go under without being even remotely aware of it.

I was not quite sure where to escape to, as the bushes above me were thorn prickled and thick and the shoreline below me was threatening to swallow me up. But I was not about to die from some tidal victimization or mere stupidity!

So here I was. It was so ironic. I'm on some beautiful tropical coast of one of Costa Rica's most amazing beaches. I had been here for just over one month searching for my purpose, looking for my niche. In this very moment, there it was, my niche, slapping me square in the face! By some will of survival, I quickly realized that there *was* no escape. I was simply at the mercy of the all-powerful ocean tide! To fight it would be futile.

It was not a conscious choice but instead a higher universal wisdom, a knowing that controlled me in that moment - and I surrendered to it. As I slumped onto a sea-salted soggy log to accept what the universe had already begun, I began to relax into it all. "If I study the waves until the tide begins to slacken", I thought, "then I can continue on." I needed to be patient and meditative, quieting my mind and my soul. It was a great exercise for me, one that I truly needed. And the universe gave it to me.

I was ashamed of the immediate restlessness in the Aries in me as it halted my meditative state to read the ocean's intentions. And there I was, quickly deserting the sea to which I had promised a commitment. I was so ashamed that I could not hold true to my word. What kind of person was I to escape to safety when I had promised the ocean I would stay and hold its hand, even if only for a few hours? I was solely disappointed in myself, my soul, and my deeper consciousness.

But forgiveness is the next step. Without it, we would surely drive ourselves into the ground and die before we have fulfilled our life's purpose. So I continued on, quickly forgiving my imperfections and fully appreciating where I was in the moment. Something about the desperation of the situation and the imminent feeling of relief and safety made me question "Why am I here?"

And then something in the air told me that I was not alone.

Last night, as I rocked in the chair with a tasty glass of chilly white wine in my sweet little Costa Rican Tico house, I couldn't help but feel a complete presence there with me. Relaxed and at ease, I glanced up to notice a gentle rocking in the chair across from me. There was a somewhat silent rhythm almost so as not to frighten me. I knew intrinsically that there was an angel, a very gentle angel, right there with me.

As I moved toward the energy in new awareness of my company, the rhythm continued. I was pleasantly surprised and emotionally astounded as tears welled up in my eyes. Who was I to deserve such an angel, and the company of three cats, and the safety of shelter from the rain storms, and the comfort of knowing I have food and drink? To top it off, who was I to deserve to have the honor of living my vision, my dream, my illusion?

Alone

Are we ever really alone? Annie is the epitome of play, Feliz is the most grumpy excuse for a cat named *'Happy'*, and Cali is a calico beauty with a mind all her own. I am so fortunate to have these three sweet feline souls in my life. I do believe I need them as much as they need me, if not more.

I was in a new country with new surroundings and challenges, and without a human companion for the first time! This was what I had wanted and, in fact, what I had longed for and dreamed of for so long. Although I felt lucky to be granted my every desire having attained this goal, I knew in that moment that I really would never be alone and that I would truly be lonely without the help of my animal companions and their company, especially now. Thinking back, perhaps that is why I sought them out, also knowing that I would be giving them a loving home. It was a perfect symbiotic relationship, where need fulfilled need. There were, in fact, many nights when I couldn't wait to get home, all because I knew I had my beautiful wonderful animal friends awaiting my arrival looking for food, love, company and more. They gave me a reason to come home.

Even with all of this love, commitment, friendship and trust, I had learned to let go of ownership and allow these living creatures to simply live. Cacao, the adventurous sailing cat, had been the complete example of the opposite, the Yin/Yang theory and a symbol of inadequate faith in the universe, trust in a greater force, as seen in our overzealous efforts to protect him. What good did our over protective insecurities do him? Couldn't we just have let him live and play? Did it really matter how much we protected him? Would the universe not take his life when it saw fit anyway? Was it really for our own good and our selfish nature of wanting to keep him around forever?

If given a chance at life, animals and all energy spirits are meant to explore and make decisions, expand their own horizons, experience adventure, pleasure, pain, boredom, and excitement. This is life, a journey of play and unknown celebrations yet to come!

I lay awake in bed at night relentlessly thinking that we are only dreaming - for we are both dreamers, he a Scorpio and me an Aries. When darkness falls, doubt can creep in. Absence of one's company can enhance that doubt in all its totality, no matter what we are.

Here I am in my own little 'tangent' town in life, more focused on this particular direction now. I wonder how and why I am here... alone.

Ever since I can remember, I have had a craving for what it would be like to be alone – I mean, really alone, completely void of any relationship. I have never known what this is like but I have so desperately sought it out, wanting to experience it. It seems a bit convoluted and dysfunctional, doesn't it? It appears as though I have been running away from everyone who ever loved me!

It seems most *normal* people want the opposite of my desires. For most, it is their lifelong dream to find a soulmate, settle down, marry and have a family – people to love and who will love back with guarantee. I have often wondered though why we, in the human condition, need to lean on someone else to attain and feel loved, adored, valued. Why can't we just lean on ourselves first and then let that true and lasting relationship just fall into place with that person who just fits into our lives like a glove? Why can't that significant other or others just be our dessert? That way, all that leaning and expectation and disappointment and hurt and possessiveness would never exist. We could then truly be as we are, sharing ourselves without jealousy, ego or resentment and shining on our own.

Time alone: There is nothing greater or more precious than this, finally learning how to love and starting all over again, starting with me. I have actually never learned how to do this, evidenced by my inability to handle a recent episode with my new neighbor from Nicaragua.

I always knew I needed to leave my marriage and delve into unknown territory in order to learn the lessons in this life that I have come here to learn. If only I had known that marriage would stir stagnation into my spirit, I would have never chosen to go that route, not for either one of us.

My lesson manifested itself profoundly one night when my space and body were violated almost to the point of rape. As frightening as it was, I knew that it was a lesson I had needed to learn on boundaries, self-respect and taking back control of my life.

Carlito was a sweet helping hand. He would do anything for a gringa (American girl). The first night I arrived in this beautiful tropical beach village of Montezuma (my supposed dream come true), it was anything but perfect! My newly acquired *carro* (slang Spanish for car) had broken down. I was on my last legs when I finally found my home, lost and frustrated late at night in a new place with two unhappy, restless, tired, over-heated felines.

When I finally arrived at my resting ground that night, Carlito was a God send and a welcome sight. He was right there to welcome me, unloading my limping jeep without hesitation.

"Mucho Gusto!" I exclaimed when I met him. This was a typical way of saying, hello, good day, nice to meet you, greetings, and thank you very much, in Costa Rica. And then those wonderful familiar formed words spilled out of his mouth, "Nice to meet you too!" He was a local sweet great looking little guy and he knew English! What a treat for a weary and tired gal from Canada!

Our friendship developed over the weeks. Carlito was always there for me. He knew every local and helped me repair my jeep back to a place where it could at least function again. I found a *bicicletta* (Spanish for bicycle) through one of his local friends to get me by in the meantime. Ironically though, every time we would venture off together to explore something new, we would notoriously find ourselves in swamp water, literally! If we weren't broken down in the middle of nowhere, we would find ourselves in desperate emotional states of desire versus anger or drunkenness and then serenity. It was crazy!

Still our friendship remained and Carlito continued to be by my side. We had loads of fun together and I actually believed I brought a little excitement into his life. But my influences also got him into drinking again. He had confessed to me that he had quit drinking for three months. I should have taken this as a sign of alcoholism. How stupid could I be? I was born to one of the same! I should have known when one boasts about halting drinking because of trouble, that it's a true sign of the disease.

As time went on, I learned this to be true, over and over again. Still I allowed it to happen. Carlito continued to help me by day. We were spending more and more time together and I was beginning to feel guilty about the time I was taking away from his wife and child, although he was not legally married.

As our friendship continued to grow, so too did our physical bond. I began to practice massage again and became inspired to dabble in it.

But when Carlito told me that he had never experienced a massage, I fell for it. How gullible could I be? It was only then that I realized he had a huge crush on me! What the hell took me so long? Did I think I wasn't adorable, attractive or tantalizing, even if only in my own unique way? Yes, I have never seen myself in this light before. A sense of intimacy began to develop and as it was not at all what I had intended, I began to fear the outcome.

Carlito began to enjoy a few wines with me in the early evening hours, which was fine. He was great company. But when he started drinking beer in the morning and sneaking rum from my fridge (I never lock my doors), I knew there was a problem far beyond my control. There were countless times when I tried to end our friendship completely. That was the only way, I thought. But when he was sober we were always such good amigos. I thought I could handle that. When he drank it was another story. It became a push and pull situation where sometimes he was sober and innocent and we could carry on being mere friends caring about friends, and other times he would get so unreasonably drunk and obnoxious that there was no reasoning with him and I would have to throw him out and lock my doors.

But the push became greater than the pull one night when he went too far! It was obvious he was blasted on cocaine with a combination of rum and whatever other substance I didn't know about. He was like a blood-sucking leech that, no matter how hard I pinched to pull him off of me, he was back for more. I even went so far as to haul him home to his wife in the midst of the night in my night gown. Despite her feeble efforts with a dim flashlight to keep him chained up, she was unsuccessful, and he followed me right back to my so-called safe haven. Although I had locked the door this time, he managed to find a way to break into the slatted glass windows and repeatedly attempted to crawl into bed with me until I became so frustrated that I threw him into the spare bedroom to let him sleep it off until day break.

As dawn broke, I awoke first and went about my morning routine, feeding the cats and cleaning the kitchen from the notorious bug fest the night before. The floors and countertops always needed a good sweep and wipe down from the swarms of life just trying to survive to the warmth of the light each night.

But there was definitely something thick in the air this morning, something different, something offensive. Carlito arose about half an hour after me. I couldn't look him the eye but I could smell the rancid odor of alcohol emitting from him from feet away. And all I could feel was separation and anxiety. As I threw his frail body out of my house that morning, telling him never to come back or to set foot on this property again, it took all the strength from within me that I could muster up, even as angry as I was with him, to watch him walk away without feeling compassion for him. I honestly felt sorry for him, his helpless addiction and his nowhere life.

I didn't see or talk to him in weeks. But as time went on, I learned to forgive him and he was able to once more look me in the eye without shame. We were able to remain friends at a distance. Eventually we were even able to play again, keeping our distance in check at all times. My fear subsided and his respect for me as a friend grew. I always hoped that one day I might be able to help him conquer his addictions to become the truth and the light and the goodness that I saw inherent in him from the start.

Revelation

I was astounded! Suddenly there was a revelation! I was sitting on my European style patio, surrounded by my feline family of three, gazing at the ocean in one direction and the directionless 360 degree view of the beautiful rainforest of Costa Rica in the other. It was a little Switzerland indeed! My apartment was small but perfect as it could comfortably house the four of us – Cali, Annie, Leo and me. (Feliz had taken off to do his own thing for a while.)

But what astounded me was that moment of realization. I had pictured myself exactly in this place barely six months ago back in Canada on a wall board vision exercise I had done with a close girlfriend who introduced me to the idea. We had spent about three hours sipping on wine and going through magazines of things we liked, things that made us feel good, places and times where and when we wanted to see ourselves. In essence, it was an exercise in discovering what we wanted and who we really were. Having the courage to then act on it and allow those dreams to unfold with faith and persistence was what this was really all about!

Today something magical was happening!

I had been through the grind to get here. My grueling sixteen hour day had consisted of challenges – late flights, lost baggage and lack of sleep, finding my way around a new city, the taxi ride to rescue my cats in a strange boarding facility, locating some Spanish speaking Tico who could help me to do all the things one could take for granted otherwise. I wondered why I had chosen a life of difficulty, a path of confusion and endless challenge. Perhaps it was because it was all part of my learning journey…and that excited me!

Ease was not what I was asking for. I had been inundated with boredom and contentment for a long time. I wanted to continue with a life full of adventure, a life that presented itself in the unknown and the daring. And so this is where I found myself.

After two weeks of searching for a car in the crime ridden streets of a third world country's capital city in which I had lived for three months, I was finally on my way to the land I had fallen in love with.

Although I had managed to squander a small legal settlement from my ex-husband (and still one of my best friends), I was still a girl of heart on a budget. My 4X4 Isuzu Trooper was as cheap as they come but still drivable. As a result, with my good Costa Rican Tico friend, whom I had hired back in San Jose, I managed to forage only one night in a broken down little town with a broken down little carro in a broken down little motel with two broken down little felines!

One must understand the pace when not living in the hustle and bustle rat race of the North American way of life. By 4:00 pm the following day, Suzy Trooper was repaired. It was time for me to go it alone the rest of the way via ferry across to the peninsula and then a relatively short drive to where I had a sweet stylish but not fancy typical Tico house awaiting.....or so I thought.

The drive to Puntarenas went without a hitch. In my broken Spanish, I bought a ticket to board me, my jeep and my two cats onto the ferry, only to find that the Tica had charged me double! For fear that I would not get on the ferry if I went back to get my money back, I passed it off and continued on. I had more urgent priorities now.

The hour and a half ferry ride was most pleasant. An attractive group of male tourists who spoke a little broken English took pleasure in showering me with beers and Spanish lessons. It was not so pleasant for the cats unfortunately as they were forced to stay in their crates. At least I could take them up from the heat and noise of the car decks for some fresh air, I thought. But as obliging as the ferry officials were, they would not allow me to take them anywhere but on the lower deck outside near the ferry's engine. As I kept a watchful eye on them while sipping on a chilly cerveza, I couldn't help but feel guilty. Still they fared much better here than down below. They were incredibly calm and grounded as if in meditation. I learned much from them that day as I watched them, trusting me and the universe, awaiting something better and knowing that they were okay.

Finally, a couple of cervezas later (yes, beer on a ferry ride!) and a keen experience of Spanish kereoke, before I knew it, the ferry was docking. All I have to do now is drive on roads that require no less than a 4X4 in the black of night with two cats to a place that I have no idea exists. No problemo!

The three of us fared pretty well - until we got lost - terribly lost! As if being lost isn't enough of a challenge in the black of night in a brand new area, to add to the mayhem, Trooper Suzy decided to challenge the evening just for a little icing on the cake! She was sounding somewhat unhealthy and as I continued to push her, I kept repeating in a mantra-like way, "Please, just last until we get there." I needed to let the fatigued cats out of their crates to stretch, relieve themselves and eat. It had been too many hours without a break for them. I too was growing weary and was beginning to hallucinate that each curve and bend in the road was another elephant. Suzy definitely needed to stop. I was pushing her as she squealed and cried and I knew that we had to stop soon before circumstances stopped us!

A Brave New World

I awoke the next morning covered in sweat with a scorpion two inches from my swollen eyes! I must admit I would love to say that I responded like a yogi out of wisdom in a calm and gentle manner, but not so this time. Immediately my arms and legs moved so fast that I swear my eyeballs followed and they all hit the ceiling in unison! By the time we had all come back down from the safety of that high place, the scorpion was gone! Now I had to find the living creepy biting crawler! I knew that when I found the creature, if I found it, I would set it free. As beautiful or ugly or indifferent as that scorpion was, it was a living thing, just like me and just like the cats. Its life meant as much to it as ours. It still wanted to live and play, and I would have no part of snuffing its life out. After all, who was I to play God and decide to stamp out its next breath? And then it was clear to me: This creature was beautiful in my own tired, terrified eyes.

So now that I had come to *that* reality, I gave my messy dirty blonde head a shake to ask myself, "Where am I?" In a daze, I quickly gave in to the scorpion and turned my attention to the other living things in my life – Feliz and Cali. After all, these two feline friends deserved some time, attention and love after such an arduous journey.

Now that I had realized that everything was okay and that we had all survived the journey, I glanced around to notice my world, so new, fresh and alive! Yes, we *had* made it! It had been a group effort. Together we did it on all of our last legs - mine, the cats' and Suzy's! So here we all were exploring our new world and soaking it all in.

It was never so clear to me as in that very moment. This journey was why we were all here! And we began to explore and play with our new surroundings as we slowly unpacked all of our treasures, including the many kitty treats I had brought, from battered and well-worn boxes and suitcases. I was pleasantly surprised by how everything had made it here all the way from Canada. Ironically though, the only unsalvageable items were two of my favorite wine glasses! To me, that was just a simple reminder to go out looking for more. What is a glass of wine without the perfect glass to spin and smell it from?

After spending the next week repeatedly attempting various methods of getting Suzy back on her feet, I felt lucky to finally find someone to temporarily band aid the problem so that I could get her into the nearest town to do some serious work.

Before I knew it, I was 4X4ing over rocks, through rivers and over pot holes. Costa Rica has some of the most amazing terrain but some of the worst roads ever! In the meantime I had bought myself a bike to get me by until Suzy was back in commission. The bike, although my favorite color of amarillo (yellow), sucked! But it was enough to get me by just to get to an area to make a phone call until my little Suzy was back in commission.

Isolation became my main focus for almost two months. Through the tears, rain and frustration, I still will not breathe or speak one word of complaint to this day. I asked for it because I deemed it necessary for my own personal growth. I fairly quickly realized though that it's not a way to live for too long, not when you need love and want to love so much. I had learned my lesson on being alone.

I suppose that's why animals came to me here. The universe recognized my loneliness and provided for me. My home became the small Spanish village's next cattery with every Tom and his "Dick" and Harry alongside to steal the kibbles freshly dispensed each morning. I must say Feliz and Cali were most patient as only a few morning cat brawls were encountered. One night I arrived home with a rodent looking kitten probably only a few weeks old. She had been abandoned by her momma and was lost in the thick of the woods. I couldn't help but pick her up and bring her home. How could I leave her out there all by herself in the dark? But with a spirit so alive, Cali and Feliz accepted her with opened hearts and she quickly became their little sister – Annie.

And so the saga began in this place they call paradise. I had to remember why I had come here in the first place. Outwardly, as most career-minded, success-driven North Americans would say, I had fled Canada and my so-called successful massage practice to seek something that was missing. I thought I might find the answer and everything would be final as soon as I found a perfect location for.... my juice bar!

I had a vision. I would open a juice shack on the beach with lively reggae music, healthy drinks and shakes, and a colorful mobile juice wagon to attract attention. I could meet all kinds of interesting passers-by in a touristy time of the season. And I would be by the ocean. I longed for that. Work would so easily become play!

Little did I know that, in time, I would be given almost exactly what I had envisioned! After nearly three months of scouring the area for a perfect location, abiding by laws and quirky legalities, nothing seemed quite right. I was beginning to give up hope. But it wasn't until I realized that it was my journey that was more important than my vision that things really began to fall into place.

I had given up on the perfect location with the perfect mobile scene on the beach. I was ready to settle for second best, at least for a little while. It wasn't until I stopped looking, trying so hard, and searching so frantically that everything began to happen. When I realized it didn't really matter what the final outcome was, it all began to take shape.

I settled for a deal with a Columbian manager who had opened up a pizza and ribs joint and was only opened in the evenings, so he was happy to have me use his facility in the daytime to help pay for the rent. The location wasn't anywhere near the beach and it wasn't really my complete vision, but heck, I figured it was a start and "Rome wasn't built in a day"! My acceptance of the new scene allowed me to let go of my efforts and expectations, knowing that I would have a place to come back to upon my return from Canada in October after the rainy season was over. When I returned, I figured I might have a few challenges but in the end everything would work itself out.

As I began to relax into the little beach town scene, I also began to meet all kinds of key people - people who would ultimately change my path in life. It's not that I lost my initial vision, it's just that because I was able to relax and let go, I could make room in my head and in my heart for new experiences and new visions.

As a result, I became a sponge open to any and all energy around me. I would notice things I hadn't when I was so caught up in finding the vehicle to my vision, fixating on *'my little life'*. Instead, my little life no longer existed and it was replaced with moment by moment experiences. I became lost in others' energies. Magically people would just seem to mesmerize me and I would, without thinking, envelope their auras into mine. Like a magnet, I would attract those people with light and likeness to me.

One day I found myself in the exact picture I had envisioned months ago, perhaps even years earlier, when I felt so strongly that something was missing. And here I was - nothing by chance! And I knew exactly where my vision board had taken me – to a little European- style accommodation, nothing too fancy, but just enough to enjoy a view of the rainforest, the ocean and the comforts of a chalet, with three cats for roommates and a perfect mobile trailer for my juice shack on the beach. All I longed for now was love and someone to share this vision with. Much to my surprise, even that was there too…just when I need it most.

Know What You Want - The Universe Will Do the Rest

Know what you want. It's all you need to know and the universe will do the rest! Sound too easy? It is! We all too often forget that life should not be a battle. If we are on the right path with perfect direction things should fall into place.

The challenging part is in the knowing what you want because it changes constantly. It's a process to keep discovering it throughout life. Seems so simple doesn't it? But it takes most of us over half our lives to put the pieces together. Then just as we have the last piece in place, we change and inevitably something better comes up. So in essence, what we want is always in flux. Once we attain one goal another one comes up. Acceptance of this process definitely makes it easier to discover what it is we want along the way. It's important to ride along with it in pleasure and with joy. If you are not feeling these feelings – pleasure, joy, happiness and a naturalness to what you are doing, chances are you may be on the wrong path.

The key is being in tune with oneself constantly. That takes effort, time and work. Many of us do not have that luxury of time simply because we do not make it a conscious priority. We are too busy raising a family, being successful in our careers, attempting to find some balance and simply just trying to survive. Consequently we find ourselves in a constant trap of a '*doing more to make more*' mentality. How many of us find ourselves so often saying, "I want to make more so I can do more in my retirement (when I am too old to really enjoy it) or leave it all behind for my children"?

For some, to know what you want takes less effort. You were born into this world and smiled upon.

"I'm going to make this easy for you", said God, "because you deserve it. You did so much thinking and working in your past life that you will easily know what you want and go forward with it in this life. And the changes will come and be dealt with gracefully throughout your life. Things will just seem to happen naturally and without much trial or error."

These are often the people who had a vision since childhood of getting married, having children and simply finding enough purpose in their role in life within their family goals. Lucky for them that life can be less complicated and less confusing with more clarity in purpose, roles and visions right from the start. It's simply just all there for them - all laid out like the pieces of a puzzle and all put together because that person wanted that from the beginning of their existence. This can happen with people who find their life's purpose in a career very quickly as well. These people just seem to know what they want and are fulfilled and connected through a divine source right from the get go. They don't question it or challenge it to change. I envy the ease these people have attained in their lives because they are living from their higher purpose.

For other more analytical types it is more of a challenge to discover what it is we truly want first. What we want can encompass everything from service, pleasure, work, play, purpose to survival, future visions and dreams. Because we are rapidly changing and so analytical, things can seem a little cloudy at times. For example, those of us who choose not to have children, or whose fate is not to have children (we don't always consciously choose our fate), often have a more difficult time realizing our true purpose as it is not clearly laid out for us. We have to take the time to figure it out.

When we are not getting what we want in our lives, perhaps we need to ask "What is it that I want? Do I really know?" Then sit down and contemplate this question. Dig deep to discover what it is that is missing. It could be doing service or it could be as simple as including more play in your life. When we dig deep and then trust in the wisdom of the universe by letting go and surrendering, what we want can freely surface with ease and gentleness. But we must first do the work and then trust. If we find that simply nothing is missing, then we most certainly must be on our own true path to joy and fulfillment in this life time because we are working from our divine light or from a God perspective.

Until I had made a vision board, I could not even begin to fathom who I really was at this point in my life or what it was that I truly could see myself doing or being. It was like I was blinded by being in the midst of it all. A vision board truly allows your thoughts and heart to flow freely in order to realize some of the subconscious things you desire to make meaning out of your life. The exercise takes away the doubt and fear that so often block us from having such revelations of the heart. A vision board or journal can help uncover what it is you truly desire deep down inside of yourself from the subconscious level and what it is you truly to deserve in any given lifetime. It does not judge or put up blocks and questions. It simply shows you where your heart is at.

To do a vision board, gather some old magazines and begin by just cutting out pictures, words, ideas, colors you like, clothing, things that make you feel good, things you have desired for a long time but have never been able to attain, things you dream of seeing and doing, things that simply make you feel happy! Paste this collection creatively onto a poster board or into a journal to remind yourself of all of your visions, whether realistic or unattainable to you at the time. It simply doesn't matter. The purpose is to help you see what you subconsciously seek and what you outwardly and openly desire. It will also help you to realize just who the real *you* is, and you may even fool yourself!

When I did my first vision board, I was running away from a marriage (an adventurous and great marriage, I might add) so that I could find what was truly missing in my life. I knew that I had lost my spark, my spirit, my light and I was hauling my partner in life down with me, so I chose to leave. He deserved more, something better....and so did I.

My vision board surprised me as I had pasted pictures of loving relationships all over it. Later, when I was able to review and contemplate my play time with the board, I was really quite astounded that I had actually found a place in my heart and wanted a loving relationship in my life. I didn't want to be *lonely*. I had only wanted to be *alone* so that I could discover myself and develop a loving relationship first and foremost with *'me'* and only then with another. I thought to myself as I analyzed this aspect of my vision board, "It must be all about timing. Perhaps I am not ready for a loving relationship right now, but someday I will be and then it will come easy. It will happen when I stop running away and embrace love for what it truly is with someone."

Sexual Connection

Sometimes the universe hands out gifts called *'angels'*. By the gifts of the universe, I was given an angel of love even before I was ready. Before I had even stopped fleeing one relationship, another potential one had come along.

He was right there, an angel I had met two years ago at the ferry terminal. We had kept in touch over the phone mostly, but every time we would cross paths in person the sparks would fly! Because universal timing dictated our fate together, two years went by during which time we somehow stayed connected through our own individual fates and our free will. We had nothing more than a mere connection and as if that wasn't enough, somehow we both knew it was more.

One evening I had invited him over for a long promised full body massage, strictly professional but because he was such a good friend I wanted to share conversation with him, a glass of wine or two and a deeper understanding of what *he* was all about. Nothing dawned on me at that point that perhaps I wanted to know what *we* could be all about, or at least I didn't care to admit it. I had offered wine to massage clients before so I thought nothing of it.

I never really felt like I was doing anything wrong. Perhaps I was in denial, but I merely felt like I deserved to have a great conversation with other great friends. Like a friend, he was always there with a listening ear and also shared of himself from time to time, just enough to keep me curious. Lending understanding so naturally and rationally, he took away any feelings of guilt I may have had for simply having a male friend to talk to and play with.

Our Kundalini energies flew that evening! Although we never partook in anything seriously sexual, we did not need to. For only a moment I simply touched his back with my belly, skin to skin, with only a hint of massage oil between us. And that was all we needed! If anyone would have entered the room at that moment, they surely would have floated immediately up into the lightness of energy and the incredible arousing ambience that we had created together!

As my unsureness and fear of doing something incredibly morally unethical crept into me and reality pervaded my body, the Kundalini energy began to dissipate, and I exited the room with somewhat less caution than when I had entered. The adrenalin was flowing and as I awaited Jay's entry into the room, I was not quite ready to respond to our new found discoveries of one another.

He came out of the room with a lightness about him, completely blissed out and with a stoned sort of look, only not on the drug stuff but instead more obviously on the sexual and emotional connectedness that he had just experienced with me. His aura was blue with a clear yellow haze around his pelvic area, and his crown chakra was mesmerized by a violet purple color. He was in a state of complete bliss from play in a sexual form.

As time became *my* reality, I gently nudged him away. My husband would be home momentarily and I was unsure as to how he might react to this whole scene and a massage booking at 11:00 o'clock and night! As he floated off, I watched in wonderment and froze into my own feelings of bliss. I wanted to be with him more now than ever!

As I stood at the front screen door and felt the warmth of the soft summer breeze on my flush face, I wondered why I was so enthralled with what had just occurred. I would not even allow for the possibility that I might be falling in love with someone else all over again. Did I even really know what love was up until now? I couldn't help but wonder that perhaps it was only a part of me that needed to play in a more intimate way and that this experience with this angel was helping me to fill that gap that I had longed for, for so long.

I had matured some almost twenty years since meeting my husband. I was only twenty-three when we met and I hadn't a clue what I wanted back then. I had a lot of growing up to do. Although I had had an awesome and adventurous relationship with him, what did this have to do with being in love? Now feelings of guilt began to set in. How could I break it to Jee that my heart was beginning to stray elsewhere because something was missing? It had been for a very long time. Now I seemed to be chasing that something, honing in on it and wanting more than ever to find it.

As thoughts began to flood my mind, some small hand of reality gently slapped me on the face and I began to adhere to the tasks at hand. I suddenly became frantic with the reality of clean up. The play session was over. Wine glasses to wash and the massage room a mess, with a twitch of my nose, my bewitched talents took care of everything in a matter of minutes! Blankets, sheets, music still playing, candles, incense and essential oils burning – like magic, all was erased from that night…and from my mind.

The scene was amazingly transformed from one of passion and heat to one of a dedicated wife anxiously awaiting her committed husband's return from his work life. And yes, *he* was committed! All the while I wanted to believe this to be true so that I could believe I was a good person and a typical little wife one hundred percent committed to her relationship. You know the kind – the woman who waits up and watches television, talks on the phone with her girlfriends and wraps her whole life around her man. Ah yes, this is a woman in love! Now how did I ever get to the point of believing in all of this mess? Certainly Jee would not have wanted me to feel this way. Now I realize, as I am older and just a little wiser (I hope), that it is part of the ill image that society strangely imposes upon couples supposedly in love.

I pretended because I didn't know any better and I didn't want to. I feared too much the result of hurting someone too deeply at the demise of *his* happiness. How could *I* deserve to be happy at the expense of some other sweet soul, someone who had given his whole life to me and his whole world? Besides that, I still did love him. Perhaps I wasn't *in love*, but wasn't *loving* enough? So I quickly put that night's experience out of my mind, out of my soul and ignored the stirring up of my Kundalini energies and all the questions that this had conjured up for me.

Jay and I went through that summer and much of fall without ever seeing each other. We would merely, by chance, bump into one another occasionally at summer markets or on the street but it was always brief. I ignored my qualms and questions and chose to avoid and deny any feelings I might otherwise have had for him or for us because I wanted to put that energy back into my marriage.

Then one cool October evening we had arranged a quick meeting, as I needed product for my massage practice, and in my denial perhaps just a feeble excuse to see him again. He had promised me an awesome jar of shea butter made specifically for me. The label read '*Molly's Own Massage Blend*'. From the moment I met him, I had always told him that I knew his products were made in love, with love. I could intuitively feel the energy in everything he made and I wanted to experience just a little taste of *his* world.

Now I had begun to stir up promises of sharing a glass of wine with him so that we could catch up on the past six months of both of our lives. Up until now, I had not even called him during that time as I was putting it all behind me. Although I had been drawn to him, my conscience told me to do the right thing. Do not follow your heart. Do not stray from your marriage. You are a bad person if you as much as begin to walk there! So simply do not!

So I didn't go there, thinking all the while that I might forget and find my inner peace and my own happiness from within. As full of passion and curiosity as I was, I would never have to walk that journey. I would discover everything in another way.

But in time my soul and innermost existence became more and more discontent, unhappy and depressed. I had always been someone known to others as carefree and happy-go-lucky, a light-hearted soul. So why was I going through such a crisis at age thirty eight? Was it perhaps a midlife crisis?

In a way, this was true. I was at a stage in my life where my mate was ready to settle down and move gracefully through *his* next stage in life. After all, he was eighteen years my senior. Why didn't I predict this? I suppose looking back, I was too much in love and believed we would always grow together ready to take on the next adventure. But he became worn out, partially because he had already lived a very full life of challenges and unknown adventures on his own, and partially because of me – high energy, restless and demanding of the world around me. I was the curious type, never stopping to take a breath and always speeding through to the next stage. My train took another track different than his, perhaps a faster one, while his began to decelerate.

I quickly discovered that timing is everything. Jee and I met at a time in life when I was asking to be rescued and he was looking for someone to rescue and take care of. He was tired of one night stands and was ready for a relationship. He and I just happened. It was perfect for that time as our needs and desires complimented each other. Although we had many beautiful years together, that time was gone and a new chapter in both our lives was beginning.

Our ambitions and goals were growing further apart with each day. We had served a purpose for each other within a fifteen year marriage and it was time to move on, perhaps not to the ending of our relationship, but to a new and healthier concept of '*us*'.

Why don't more people recognize and consider the inevitability of change when they so willingly give of their souls to a partner for not a year, or ten, or even twenty, but a lifetime in marriage? We clearly set ourselves up for disappointment when our paths do not merge for life because we change in ways that are unpredictable and often not complimentary to our partner's changes. A crisis inevitably sets in, inducing relentless and unnecessary guilt, most often ultimately resulting in divorce. What we fail to realize in our own human civilization is that marriage is a man-made concept that sets its trap and takes a leg hold on us for life leaving us coiled in the chains of entrapment, often times creating a sense of despair and lack of hope. Ultimately many people stay in relationships because they see no alternative and it's always more difficult to leave and step out of that comfort zone into a world of unknowns. For many, the status quo of numbness of spirit and even misery at times seems much easier to cope with than the option to change. Accepting one's fate and carrying on in a gray and lifeless marriage is where many people inevitably stay – trapped and stuck forever. I say to anyone who is living in the bondage of such a relationship and anyone who wonders what life is really all about, let go of your fear and take hold of the courage that is inside of you. You just might be surprised what you might find on the other side!

Now I am not saying that one cannot be happy and fulfilled in a union of marriage. For some, a marital relationship can last a lifetime and bring much joy and playfulness to both people because they are changing together gracefully. But for so many who live in quiet desperation, years may go by - unhappy, discontented years of living in a world of simple acceptance of '*what is*'. Don't you know that *you and you alone* have so much potential of being more and celebrating life in a world of joy because *you* are beautiful and special and *you* are deserving of that? Accepting of '*what is*' is actually very healthy. It only becomes unhealthy when that acceptance creates unhappiness from within because the light inside of you is being subdued and ignored. If you are living your light within your relationship, hats off to you! But if you are living in your shadow, then it can truly hold you back from experiencing the true joy that is there for you to take hold of, the life that *you* have every right to live!

Humanity

I have often wondered what my life might be like if I had no other human influence and was living in a box void of any communications or existence with other human beings. How would I play? Who would respond and hear my laughter? How could I learn from experience and interaction? I have even gone so far as to try to live that reality, thinking perhaps I would come to some revelation, some sort of enlightenment.

But it only led me to a deeper desire to understand our human existence and our purpose in life. So why *do* we exist? Why *are* we here - to collect wood, start a fire, meditate - on what? And who might you share your enlightenments with should you meditate to such a degree? Who might you benefit or affect - anyone or no one? What would be the purpose if you could not share what you have been bonked on the head to share with those souls or vibrations of energy ready to accept your learnings and help to evolve the world?

It all comes down to purpose. It is not only our purpose that creates the desire to surround ourselves with other physical beings, be they humans, animals or plants, but perhaps it is also a calling towards something that makes us feel like we belong in an otherwise world of feeling lost and alone.

What would life be like without sound, music, energy, vibration, without others' voices to hear, to talk to, to play with? Why do we have the blessed five senses of taste, touch, smell, sight and sound?

We are, as physical beings, meant to explore all of these gifts of the senses. We are meant to be joyous and celebratory for these pleasures that have been given to us by the gracious giving nature of the universe!

Today was amazing - a totality of my thoughts in true action! The day was set to be completely tainted by a tropical storm. Although I had fully accepted it and I had even invited its beauty and mysterious power, I knew this time I could not stay inside the comfort of my sweet warm and dry little apartment curled up with my warm and fuzzy now seven felines - not this time. I had my juice bar to run and I had to tend to it.

I had hired two young and eager American girls to give me some reprieve from the Shack after having been there too many long hours during the first two weeks of opening to ensure everything was happening on course. Even though Costa Rica is probably *the* most modern developing country in Central America, it is still not without its challenges, especially when doing business. Water shortages and electricity cut offs are difficult obstacles to overcome when you are trying to please a daily crowd of expecting Americans and Europeans. I can't say I blame them. After all, they were on vacation.

But today was somehow different. Today the universe had expectations. It was obviously time to put things on hold, perhaps to prevent us from getting too off track, too greedy, which frequently seems to be our nature as human beings. And so the universe decided to show its powerful face as it poured rain, tormenting down, leaving many wanderers stuck on streets and trapped in flooded homes. What had just the day before been a bustling little village filled with smells of garlic wafting from specialty restaurants and spicy aromas from new age incense shops with hammocks and beach wraps, was now suddenly transformed into a deserted water drenched space void of sights and sounds. It seemed the universe was about to teach human kind a lesson or two and show us what truly is important in living.

I had been feeling a bit sorry for myself, missing my family and friends from back home and the ease of ever day life and business there. I was fatigued from a couple of tough weeks of burning the candle at both ends. I was feeling loveless, void of sensual pleasures, passionless and missing sweet conversation. I was feeling rather insignificant in my significant others' life as he was back in Canada making the best of what was necessary there in the moment. To top it off, I had an albeit superficial but ugly burn on my wrist from trying to hurriedly make coffee at my juice bar, a result of stress, and I had somehow accumulated a host of red dots all over my body due apparently to fleas from having an overabundance of feline friends in my life! Come to think of it, I think I also had developed an uncomfortable case of ringworm on my back from working with and rescuing too many bush animals!

Today though, I taught my own self a lesson, or rather the universe decided to follow up on my thoughts. As far as what is important today, I could see clearly that we are all struggling and many times desperate to make our way in life with what we know or do not know, and what we are presented with in any given moment.

I just wanted so badly to appease my own comforts and do the minimum to close down the Shack in an obvious stormy circumstance so that I could head back to my cozy apartment and nurse all of my physical and emotional wounds. I hadn't the energy or confidence to do much of anything today. So when I arrived at the Shack, I could not believe my eyes! We were in the midst of a torrential tropical storm, in fact, almost a hurricane, and my juice bar stood with its '*Open*' sign out! I wondered where the common sense in humanity had gone in that moment, and I found myself feeling a little annoyed. Why weren't they closed?

But when I hurriedly marched in to reprimand whomever had lingered long enough to be paid to stay opened, I immediately realized from what I saw that I had been wrong and perhaps too quick to jump the gun. Here were two people, one sweet girl I had hired and an elderly man, in fact, a regular and committed customer. They were sitting and having a calm conversation in amongst the chaos, rain and noise. More than half the town had closed down and here was this newly opened pitiful little juice bar, still sitting there with its *abierto* (Spanish for *open*) sign hung out. The lights were on and no one was home, except two playful spirits just enjoying being there. It was something most beautiful to behold - two people who were totally unaware of the chaos around them and more in the midst of their own bliss than any physical chaos that was happening in that very moment!

My ego couldn't help but tell me that I somehow had something to do with creating this beautiful scene. But then I snapped into it and realized that it had nothing to do with *me* – it was the universe working through me, and I realized just moments later that I was merely a tool.

As I had left my tiny abode just moments earlier in a bit of a frantic rage in the peak of the storm, my tiny apartment was flooding and I felt a sense of urgency to return as quickly as possible. I knew I had to tend to the Shack and I knew the felines were all okay at home. I had everything under control - towels wrapped by the doors and buckets out to catch the leaks. The faithful seven would surely be okay until my return. After all, I would only be gone an hour to close down the Shack and then I would vehemently return to my little family.

But I quickly discovered that another family was awaiting me at the Shack. Not only had I arrived there in the midst of a very wet storm, but I do believe my unnecessary urgency snapped a few people in this vacation paradise back to a sense of reality. I suppose it was my survival mode that had kicked in, perhaps a little overzealous, but I had endured the worst of storms on the rough seas in a tiny sailboat with little experience, and I wasn't about to let this one catch me by surprise!

A long story short, my somewhat urgent arrival onto the scene was complimented by the onset of a more aggressive downpour and a bit more of a crisis witnessed by impassable river routes and stranded buses to smaller outlying villages. This, in turn, created a further crisis in the eyes of local tourists whose expectations were to somehow end up safely in the comforts of their abodes at the end of the day. Many were surprised and most just simply were oblivious to the intensity of what a storm like this might bring. It's a funny phenomenon: When people are on vacation, especially in foreign lands, they become desensitized to natural disasters and just keep vacationing! It's like reality escapes them as they become numb to any possibility of having their vacation ruined.

It seemed fallen upon my plate, whether I willed it or not, to take responsibility to help get these otherwise stranded people home so that they could take comfort in their safety and surroundings for the night. Without hesitation, and with only a clairvoyance that the universe had bestowed upon me, once more I became a tool for

human help. When my little Suzy Trooper was void of all passengers, I was quickly rewarded by my own safe arrival to a home that had somehow miraculously dried up of all of the water and flooding I had left behind. My family of felines was eagerly awaiting my return.

As I reflected on my day that evening, I knew that this was just another '*thought –proven- true- to life-in the -living of it*" experience! Thank you, Universe, for giving me an invaluable lesson in slowing down and living in the moment.

Just Another Ordinary Day

Thank God for a new day! For every new day brings hope, change from the day gone by. And we are left with the now, today, the moment. Call it Monday mayhem! Everything is relative here in this physical world. If we couldn't learn lessons and see signs from a single moment of experience, then what would be that moment's purpose?

Feliz had been missing for almost 3 days now. He had disappeared just prior to the tropical storm and so was out there somewhere in the mayhem. Frankly, though, I was not worried. He had done this before for much longer - a month in fact - and always managed to find his way back, even if carried by angels!

Monday was like a mad continuum of Sunday, only more in a 'tormenting- of- my- life' kind of way. As insignificant as it all seems now, I couldn't help but question the laws of karma. I suppose I had already been rewarded for my service yesterday and today was simply that – a new day to prove my goodness, and perhaps practice my patience and wisdom once again.

I awoke to a flat tire, a lost cat and a list of impossibilities a mile high! My thoughts bewildered me as I thought, "Realistically, how will I ever tackle the day?" But as I slowly meditated and sank into the moment, I began to know that none of it really mattered. Instead what mattered was how I dealt with the demands of the day, the hour, the moment!

The Calm After the Storm

Life will go on and on. Because we are energy beings, we never die. And so too will a story if the writer allows it to. It's time to end this one and begin another. A book is only a chapter, each page meant to be turned at the reader's pace, and then....it is time for a new creation.

Move on. It is the moment that is meant to be lived – now! Life is too short to lament or grieve for too long. If you need to grieve, grieve. Then relax and surrender. The universe and all of your angels want for you to move on to find purpose, fulfillment, energy, direction, joy and aliveness in everything you do. A journey is not without challenges, for if our journeys were perfect and exactly what we envisioned, they would not be journeys. Instead, they would be paintings of perfect portraits, predictable and unanticipated, hanging lifelessly on the wall.

I leave you with this. Enjoy *your* journey, for it is a gift given uniquely to *you.* Remember to love along the way, laugh often and dance (somebody once said) like no one is watching. I chuckle when I write this as I so often do this in the comfort of my own personal surroundings, sometimes even with a glass of wine or two to help me lose my inhibitions and unwind. I have sometimes thought about what might happen if I practiced my dance on the beach or some place where people might actually see me and reach out wanting to share because they are one with the feeling I get when I dance! Would it be as I think? That the energy of play would be simply contagious? Yes, everyone can feel this passion!

Whether we are ready to feel the passion or not, we are here to live our lives within the process of evolution. If we can make a difference in whatever we may see as our missions of importance on our own individual journeys, then we have fulfilled our purpose. We need not try to "build Rome in a day" or change the world in a lifetime. I have to tell myself this every day. We are merely here as infinite energy beings, curious as we may be and defined in our goals and roles in the physical world. We need to do what we may and then release ourselves, for this universe is much too massive for us to think we can control anything or everything about it – personally and universally.

In the meantime, living well and finding purpose through service to those around us and within our communities are keys to finding deeper happiness. Experience as you will the world to a greater degree, always learning and discovering more and new, whether it be through traveling, reading, having children and grandchildren, rescuing animals, or simply just touching the souls of those who may be less fortunate than you or all whom you come into contact with. What matters more is that you know that *you* can make a difference in everything and every action you take in life – moment to moment, day to day, week to week. *You* can make a difference simply in the way you choose to live your life.

Strive not to be perfect, but instead act whenever you are able with compassion and understanding. When you are able to let go of the mind and act from the gut, you will find that unconditional love and ease of life will naturally fall into place. Your goals and visions will align with everything you dream possible, but not until you are acting on behalf of a much larger picture and driven by the divine, not the ego. Only then, when you stop to take a good look at your motives for your actions, will you accomplish something amazing and beautiful! When *you* shine, you allow others to shine!

Always remember to play! It will set your attitude and your spirit to soar with a positive spin throughout your whole life. See how a smile can make you feel different on an otherwise challenging day. Someone once said, "Man is most comical when he takes himself too seriously". This life of yours is not a dress rehearsal. Embrace it, enjoy it and celebrate it, with honesty, integrity and love!

Circles of Healing

I sobbed, I cried, I felt, I lied. I'm blessed, confused....
I feel....everything...nothing.....
Sadness....love.... emotion.... thoughts....

Two years have passed since I began my healing journey with this journal. In some ways time stands still. All the feelings of confusion and joy, grief and sadness, fear and love that I possessed then have not somehow magically vanished. No, in fact, they are there more than ever now as part of my deep rooted soul existence and awareness. I am just now beginning to deal with them with an attitude of acceptance rather than resistance. These feelings, emotions and thoughts, rational or irrational, will always be there, as long as the sun continues to shine and the ocean changes with the tides. As long as we exist as energy in the physical world, they will ever be.

Learning to accept *'what is'* is a large part of any healing journey. When we can master this concept of acceptance and relinquish our illusionary control, somehow the fear fades and love magically replaces it. Life can then become a playground full of games of adventure and eager anticipation of what is to come.

Finally, believe in yourself and that anything is possible. Having faith in a higher power is one thing, but to know that you *are* divine in your right and you can do whatever it is you set your mind to, is quite another! Knowing what you want at any given time, and then being able to flex with the wind, can certainly help unlock the door to your own enlightenment. You will be surprised at how easily things will begin to happen when you are working hand in hand with a divine source. You will know you are on the right track to living your life's purpose because the universe will be providing answers and guiding you every step of the way, and you will clearly recognize it.

So let the fun begin! Let go and surrender your soul to a faith that will carry you beyond your wildest imaginations! Feel everything - your breath, your senses, your life....love. And then keep going. Nothing can hold you back now!

We are all here on our own healing journeys - from the moment we left the safety of the womb to the hour of contemplation of what we have done with our time here on Earth. The going *will* get tough at times. It always does. Move gently through it. Be soft but strong. Never lose sight of the love that surrounds you. Embrace it. Then move on...with strength and courage.

I can see clearly now! Life is what happens at play! I'm going now.... to play my own game...to shine my own star! See you in the sky!

Bibliography

Beattie, M. (1992). *Codependent No More.* Center City, MN: Hazelden.

Brennan, B. A. (1987). *Hands of Light.* New York, NY and Toronto, ON: BANTAM BOOKS, A division of Random House, Inc.

Dyer, Wayne. (2015). *Understanding the Power of the words, I AM, Free Video Series, Video 2.* Hay House Publishing.

Gilbert, E. (2010). *Committed.* New York, NY: VIKING, Published by the Penguin Group.

Hicks, E. a. (2004). *Ask and It Is Given.* Carlsbad, California: HAY HOUSE, INC.

Millman, D. (1984, c1980). *Way of the Peaceful Warrior.* Tiburon, Calif; Emeryville, CA: H.J. Kramer, Inc;Emeryville, CA: Distributed by Publisher's Group West. .

Tolle, E. (2008). *Oneness With all Life.* New York, NY: DUTTON, The Penguin Group.

About the Author

Hannah Lee doesn't write for a living. She lives to write! For years, it has been her all-time favorite past time, from journaling her challenges and aha moments, to composing newspaper articles and local community press releases, to documenting letters and petitions to political figures for affecting positive change for animal welfare and other environmental causes. She has also created and developed numerous websites for new and existing businesses including her own. Whatever it is that she writes, it's always from the heart! After having edited some of her own friends' work, this book has been her inspiration to become a published author herself.

"Life is What Happens....At Play" is aimed at awakening those ready to realize the absence and importance of play in their busy lives and how to reintegrate it back into their realities on a daily basis to foster and encourage the child within. Her reference to Dr. Stuart Brown's National Play Institute was a major influence in writing this book.

Hannah's writing style is one that reflects who she is. She is an empath with an overabundance of compassion and respect for all life. She holds a Bachelor of Social Work undergrad degree and practiced in the field for three years, working with homeless and mentally ill populations, crisis centres, and crime prevention education. When asked, "Why did you choose social work?" Hannah says that she really didn't know what she wanted to do professionally after graduating from high school, but she knew one thing was for certain – she definitely wanted to fulfill her purpose in this life by making a difference in the world.

One of Hannah's many great passions is traveling. She was a flight attendant for eight years and admits that it was a lot of fun! Besides that, she says that travel allows us to "be in the moment" and seize opportunities to be of service as the universe requires of us. Hannah whole heartedly admits that she was more compelled to help her human and animal brothers and sisters while traveling, and she had ample opportunities to do so.

Her 2-year sailing sabbatical, beginning at the Inside Passage to Alaska and ending in the Caribbean Sea, took her on one adventure after another. "It literally changed my life and how I look at everything now", says Hannah. "I can take things with a grain of salt a lot more when the going gets tough. Many times I thought I had had my last day out there in the dark of night and in the rolling high seas. One thing is for certain, that particular adventure definitely made me stronger and instilled in me a belief that I can do or be anything I so desire. If I can sail and live to tell about it, I can do anything! The whole experience was a highlight of my life!"

Hannah's work in the healing arts has taken her on another journey of healing and helping her animal and human companions. She has practiced energy healing, massage, body work and other intuitive healing therapies for the past ten years. Hannah works through her animal spirit guides to communicate with animals on all levels. As this book is being published, Hannah is already working on a second book to be part of a children's literature collection entitled, "Can You Hear the Animals?" This project is aimed at helping young readers to develop that same sense of empathy, compassion, love and respect for all life that Hannah feels so deeply and carries with her in all she does.

Hannah enjoys nature in the form of animals, gardening, hiking, and long walks along the ocean or in the rainforest. She lives on North Vancouver Island with her partner in life and a frenzy of animal family members. They live in rural setting with an abundance of wildlife always around to keep life interesting!

Lightning Source UK Ltd.
Milton Keynes UK
UKOW01f1024230218
318381UK00001B/335/P

9 781504 343244